Life Without
POINT GUARD

Life Without *My* POINT GUARD

DENIS HODGE

authorHOUSE®

AuthorHouse™
1663 Liberty Drive
Bloomington, IN 47403
www.authorhouse.com
Phone: 1-800-839-8640

Published by AuthorHouse   11/27/2012

ISBN: 978-1-4772-7415-6 (sc)

Any people depicted in stock imagery provided by Thinkstock are models, and such images are being used for illustrative purposes only.
Certain stock imagery © Thinkstock.

This book is printed on acid-free paper.

Because of the dynamic nature of the Internet, any web addresses or links contained in this book may have changed since publication and may no longer be valid. The views expressed in this work are solely those of the author and do not necessarily reflect the views of the publisher, and the publisher hereby disclaims any responsibility for them.

Acknowledgements

Many people helped make this book possible, but I would like to especially thank a few. Any of the English teachers from my scholastic past would agree that I need to thank God because it was surely through divine guidance that I was able to publish a book. I want to thank Chris Evans for being so positive and helpful in editing and helping get the book to print. I want to thank Gina Brown for proofing my spelling and grammar. She has laughed at my spelling for years and some things never change. Nathan Boone, one of the first players I coached at Crittenden County, proofed the book and provided honest opinions. He is one of the most intelligent and driven men I know. Thank you. Lastly, I want to thank local teacher and one of my fellow church deacons, Todd Merrick, who spent hours reading and proofing the book. With help from these and many others, this project was made possible.

Introduction

On June 20, 2008, my son and I had the perfect day for both of us. Jake was going into the seventh grade and we were having summer football workouts. Jake was a four-sport athlete, loved life and loved to play anything where there was competition. His favorite sport was basketball. Although drawn toward most physical activity, Jake didn't like to lift weights or work on the farm. Among my various duties as a high school teacher was serving as the strength and conditioning coach for the football team. On that particular June morning we had a scheduled weightlifting period at the high school gymnasium.

Jake and I were at the school by 9 a.m., to work out with the team. I remember asking our varsity tailback if he thought Jake would ever be my lifting partner. We both just laughed because Jake, like most young men, liked to look in the mirror, but lifting was something he could do without. Shortly after getting to the gym that morning, it began to rain, and rain hard. It was a godsend for Jake because he was going to have to drive a tractor and help me rake hay that afternoon.

With the rain falling, his attention quickly turned to a young lady friend who he'd been interested in for quite some time. That night, there were plans for having dinner with her and some of her family. The rain meant he could concentrate on prepping for a 12-year-old's date instead of sweating on the farm with dad. I can still see Jake grinning from ear to ear, shaking his fist at his side in joy as thunder clapped and the ground became soaked with a nice summer rain. Knocked out of work in the hayfield, Jake and I went to Dairy Queen for lunch where he ate the biggest ice cream cone I have ever seen. Afterward, we went home and hung out together at the house. That evening he kept the much-anticipated date with his new little female friend, Kathryn.

Also that evening, my wife Shannon, the high school girls' basketball coach, and my daughter Jessi, the point guard on the team, had a summer league game in Murray, a town just over an hour's drive from home. It was an uneventful evening, and following the basketball game, Shannon picked up Jake from his dinner with Kathryn and her family, who are good friends of ours. They talked a bit on the way home. Jake told her he'd had a great time. When they got home, Jake kissed his mother and went to bed. It had been a late evening with the game out of town, getting home and gathering up the family. It was about 1:30 a.m. when Jake went to sleep. He was out in a hurry, but that wasn't unusual because he always could fall asleep fast, especially after a long day like that.

What happened that night changed my life forever. I was letting everyone sleep a little longer than normal because we'd been so late the night before. My dad and I were out on the farm working when he got a call on his cell phone. He hung up and told me "Go to the house, it's Jake." When I got there, I found that my daughter Jessi had gone downstairs to wake up Jake to watch a movie with her. She found him lifeless in his bed. The next few hours were a blur. The emotional trauma for my family was overwhelming.

In the coming days and weeks, we would long for an answer. It was very important to know why our son had died. Despite an extensive medical examination, doctors and the coroner were unable to give us a specific reason. His heart had stopped, they said.

I have learned that many things in this life are unpredictable. I have no regrets about my relationship with God, my son and my family. I have the greatest friends and family on earth. Without them, I don't know how we would have gotten through the first days, weeks or months after Jake's death. What I have come to know even more certainly is that we humans on God's earth are part of something much larger than ourselves. We are part of something of divine origin and of God's design and plan. I have learned that it's okay to laugh and it's okay to cry. The following is our story. I have also included stories of real life lessons I have experienced that will help raise our children to leave a powerful and positive legacy.

CHAPTER 1

Leave A Legacy

You are reading this text because grief can manifest itself in many forms—it can be disabling or inspiring. Grief can come from the loss of a job, a break up, a missed opportunity. Grief is different for everyone. The thesis of this book is based on the legacy of my 12-year-old child, whose life and death will not be in vain. Through the strength and support of our family and friends, my wife Shannon and I have pledged to give meaning to Jake's life and his untimely death. Through a testament of morality and faith, Shannon and I are using our unique perspective on life and death to enrich the lives of others. We believe that we are so qualified because we have experienced something that no parent, grandparent, friend or community should have to endure—the untimely death of a young, vibrant boy—the loss of our only son.

Jake died in his sleep early on a Saturday morning in June 2008. The cause of his death was never determined. His heart simply stopped beating. Jake had a heart so filled with love, faith and thirst for the future that the pain of his passing wrapped its dark hands around all who knew him. Fortunately, those same qualities that made Jake a terrific young athlete and devout Christian, strengthened and tempered our spirit. I have been led to do three things: establish a scholarship foundation, create an outreach program and publish this book.

As parents who have lost a child, we have learned to cope with grief, to channel our emotions in order to preserve the lasting legacy of our son's life. Through our personal insight, we long to influence the lives of others, to help parents and grandparents better understand the things in life that are truly lasting and genuinely important. It is our desire that, through this book, we might provide ideas and answers on dealing with moral and ethical issues that young people in all walks of life encounter. Through these words and wisdom, we hope to improve the mental and physical well being of others by sharing our story and revealing what we believe are sound moral judgments based on Christian values and a unique perspective of life and death.

So many times parents devote countless hours and thousands of dollars preparing their offspring for things they will encounter in this earthly life. We push them to excel in athletics, to study for the ACT and teach them how to get a driver's license. We are all guilty of encouraging our children in so many areas that we fail to prepare them for the one thing that is inevitable and real—death.

A few months before our son's death, he was talking with his mother and revealed that he was scared of dying. Fortunately, my wife is a very strong and spiritually enlightened woman. She lay down with Jake, prayed with him and explained to him that death is not to be feared if we have lived our life according to God's plan. It would have been so easy for her to have said, "Jake, you're not going to die." But she didn't. The great gift of immortality is achievable through the grace of our redeeming Savior as spelled out in the gospels. If we have prepared our mortal souls for the inescapable reality of death, then our short experience on earth will have meaning. Every day I am thankful for my Christian wife and the way she handles what are difficult situations.

As parents, Shannon and I have absolutely no regrets about the way our son lived his life. Certainly, we wanted him to long outlive us. Other than that, Jake's legacy is just what we wanted it to be. The only thing we would have chosen differently was the length. Our son embodied goodness and wholesomeness, and he possessed a competitive spirit that provided him with an intestinal fortitude so very uncommon in pre-teens.

There is a story that has been repeated several times about Jake playing a pickup basketball game with some other young boys and some young adults. One of the older fellows was cursing and ranting about issues that arose during the game. Jake took the ball, held it under his arm and told the foul-mouthed opponent this: "It doesn't take much of a man to use those types of words, but it takes a very big man not to." As parents we love to hear stories like this one in reference to our children. Athletic, academic and social accomplishments are great, but to someone who lost his child, it is most important to know he was a Christian and he was a good person.

Yes, Jake excelled in athletics. He was a national qualifier in youth rodeo; he was well known for his play on the baseball diamond, the basketball court, and running with a football. But more importantly, Jake excelled in life. He was an excellent student, community volunteer and highly respected among his fellow middle schoolers. Though it is human nature, we should not ask to know why he was taken so soon, but to learn from his life and to use his life to help others physically, financially and spiritually. For such a young man, he casts a very long shadow.

We must not focus all of our energy on finding a reason for this tragedy. We must have faith that somehow there is indeed a design to it all. In life, we are not guaranteed fairness. Just like when we hear that called third strike and step out of the batter's box. We go back to the dugout and have faith that it will be made right at some point later in the game.

Sports do not build character, they reveal it. In sports, Jake made his teams better. His drive and passion lifted teammates and caused them to elevate their own play. He made his school better by showing that a young boy with seemingly everything going for him could also be courteous, obedient and studious most of the time. He made his community better because he embodied the very genius, faith and talent that make us all proud. Death will not stop a spirit like Jake's, and we are here to make sure that his legacy is used in the way God intends. As you read this, you too are surely called to not only leave your legacy, but to use the life of a loved one to motivate you to make this world a better place.

Through this text, it is our prayer that you will find comfort and reason. We encourage you to dream with your children, spend time with them, and never take them for granted. For all of us, including our children, there is a point where our lives end and our legacy begins. What legacy do you want for yourself, and what legacy do you want for your children?

CHAPTER 2

Life is not a Game

In this life, we are forced to accept certain things that may cause us discomfort or pain. I never liked accepting anything that remotely looked or smelled like defeat. I grew up wanting to win at everything. Thanks to God's blessings, I was a pretty good athlete in high school. Due to a number of my outstanding teammates, we won a Kentucky state championship in football in 1985, my senior season at Crittenden County High School in Kentucky.

After high school, I played baseball at Southeast Illinois Junior College in Harrisburg, and then later at Eastern Kentucky University in Richmond, where as a junior, I hit .344 and was third in batting average in the Ohio Valley Conference. I started thinking that I was pretty good. You need to know also, that my senior year in college my hitting coach got a job at another school, my favorite bat was lost, my average went south, and I went to the bench. It was the best lesson I learned in sports because it helped me to understand how to coach players who don't always get to play. As a coach, this painful lesson has paid off for me many times. Several of the relationships I have made with players have been with the player who was not an everyday starter.

My wife, Shannon, on the other hand, has never had to experience the pine. She was a standout athlete in high school and went on to become a Division III All American basketball player at Centre College, where she is still the all-time leading scorer. She has a powerful inner will and is a true competitor with grit and guts like no other woman I know.

After college I did something that most sensible thinking people questioned. I enlisted in the U.S. Army. I had a college degree in my hand and could have gone right into the job market. Instead, I joined the Army, not as an officer, but as an enlisted man. I felt that I owed something to my country. The military didn't owe me anything, but I had a debt to pay and wanted to get that done before I moved on with my professional life.

Shannon and I married in the summer of 1991, right before I left for basic training. By January of 1992, we were living on base at Fort Drum, N.Y. The best that I can remember, it was 40 below and hip deep in snow.

The military was always full of new and exciting challenges. Some were pretty cool and some not so cool. One of the things I liked about the military was that they didn't care who you were, where you were from, or the color of your skin. If you worked hard, there was always an opportunity for new challenges. I went through Ranger, Airborne and Air Assault training within the first two years of my service. My uncle sent me a letter while I was in Ranger training. He was a World War II veteran of Normandy and the Battle of the Bulge. In his letter, he told me that he respected my courage, but questioned my judgment. Today, we do such a good job of being grateful to our troops. Our veterans are honored and held in high regard by the general public. As a veteran, this gives you a wonderful feeling; but being able to serve my country in Uncle Sam's army has done more for me as a person than I did for him as a soldier.

Competition has always been a driving force in my life. Whether it was playing high school football, collegiate baseball or seeking higher achievement in the military, I have always been motivated to compete. I wish this had carried over more to the classroom when I was younger. As I grow older, I have come to the realization that I don't love winning that much, but I hate losing. At this point in my career, the greatest part of winning is seeing the excitement of kids and parents as they accomplish something together.

I admit that losing is one of the worst things I have ever felt. Losing my son was, and still is, the deepest pain I have ever experienced. Unlike a game, where the hurt soon fades away, this loss is slow to fade at all. It's so funny that when kids are little, you can just take them to McDonald's and life is good again. For those of you who have lost a loved one, you know that at times, even years later, the loss comes back to the pain you felt the day after. For some people, this may happen every day. For some it may happen once a week. Everybody deals with loss differently. Some deal well early and then struggle later. Others struggle early and deal better over time.

When my son Jake died unexpectedly in June 2008, I experienced emotions that I never knew existed. I was forced to swallow the greatest loss of my life. It was and still is an excruciating, helpless feeling. There was nothing I could do about it. I was solely at the mercy of this natural world and its painful truths of life and death.

In the first hours after Jake's death, all I could do was walk up and down my driveway. I cried a lot and prayed more. I put my full faith in God's hands and sought direction. I found no joy, no happiness, but an inner peace that is unexplainable.

Like any parent in a situation like that, Shannon and I were lost and devastated. But on that driveway the night of my son's death, I gave God my full attention. It was during those brutal hours right after my son's death that God gave me a clear vision about which direction to take. The first concept we have to understand is that we are on this earth to glorify God. That may mean in victory, or that may mean in defeat. If we do not grasp this concept, we thank God for all good things and blame him for all bad things.

My prayer is that no one reading this book will outlive their children. But if you do, know that God has a plan for you, too. What God told me to do was simple. He wanted me to be more in tune with the needs of others, with the needs of my family, and to become victorious in a spiritual sense. He told me that Jake's death would not be in vain. He told me to reach out to others.

The first thing I knew I had to do was speak at my son's funeral. I believed that I was the only one who could fulfill the promise of Jake's legacy. After much prayer and consideration, I came up with the words to share at my son's funeral. The following is a small portion.

> "My life has been blessed beyond measure. I live in the greatest country in the world. I live in the greatest community in the world. I am blessed with the best friends a man could ever hope to have in two lifetimes. My mom and dad and family are the greatest blessings a man could ever hope for. I married my high school sweetheart, who is the most beautiful woman in the world—and the best mother a child could ever have. She gave me the two most wonderful children in the world. I serve a living God who is always there, even when I am too busy to listen. But today God has my attention."

The second way we have given meaning to Jake's legacy and dealt with his death is to first start a scholarship foundation. The Jake Hodge Foundation grants educational scholarships to students who display honesty, character, and integrity in their actions. The foundation rewards students who excel in the classroom and in their chosen fields of competition. Students are forever challenged to lead a purpose driven life and leave a legacy. And thirdly, anytime I am given the opportunity to speak to people about my faith, I will do so.

CHAPTER 3

Decisions for a Lifetime

My wife was born in 1966 in Marion, Kentucky. She was a great athlete as a young girl. Back then there were few sports for girls only. She played baseball and football with the boys.

When we first met as young children, it was certainly not love at first sight. In fact, Shannon despised me. She was in sixth grade and I was in fifth. We were in line to be issued football equipment for our local league. Shannon loves to tell this story, and I don't think there is a kid in the Crittenden County school system who has not heard it from her. For some reason on that day, I felt the need to say, "Girls can't play football." In hindsight, this was a big mistake. She turned around and gave me a body slam that would have made Hulk Hogan proud. And to this day, kids still come up to me and say, "Did Mrs. Coach Hodge really slam you?" It took a few years, but I convinced her to like me somewhat. Shannon went on to have a great high school career in basketball and track.

Shannon graduated from high school in 1985. She was recruited to play basketball for Centre College, a private liberal arts college in Danville, Kentucky. Centre is one of the top liberal arts colleges in the nation. Danville is a small town of about 18,000. It was recently featured by Time magazine as one of the nation's outstanding small towns. Centre gained national attention in 2000 for hosting a Vice

Presidential debate. Centre is a great institution and has had many famous graduates, including Cawood Ledford, who was the voice of the Kentucky Wildcats for many years. Two United States Vice Presidents, Adlai Stevenson and John C. Breckinridge, were also educated there, as was E.A. Diddle, a legendary basketball coach at Western Kentucky University, and Congressman John Y. Brown Sr., whose son, John Y. Brown Jr, you may know, was governor of Kentucky in the 80s, while married to former Miss America and CBS sportscaster Phyllis George.

Shannon studied economics at Centre and played on the women's basketball team where she scored 2,000 points—never made a three-point shot—and was a Division III All American. To this day, she remains the leading men's and women's scorer in Centre's basketball history. She also holds others records at Centre and led the Lady Colonels to the NCAA final four in 1989.

After graduating from Centre in 1989, she went to Western Kentucky University in Bowling Green, Kentucky to work on her master's degree. At Western she was a graduate assistant to the Lady Toppers basketball program. The winning ways continued as the Lady Toppers also went to a sweet 16 while Shannon was coaching there. While at Centre, Shannon was coached by Lea Wise Prewitt, quite possibly the greatest female coach in Kentucky basketball history. And at Western, she coached with the legendary Paul Sanderford. So her coaching success at Crittenden County comes as no surprise.

I played three sports in high school, but ended up sticking with baseball in college. For two years, my post-secondary education was close to home in Harrisburg, Ill. Baseball at Southeast Illinois College allowed me to get a handle on college studies and to play ball. The only four-year college interested in me after that was Trevecca Nazarene University in Nashville, Tennessee. There, I met Coach Elliott Johnson. I only played one semester under Coach Johnson, but he had a profound affect on my life. Coach Johnson was at Trevecca for 11 years and had 10 winning seasons. He has since coached elsewhere and in 2008 the Fellowship of Christian

Athletes awarded him the Jerry Kindall Character in Coaching Award. He is also the author of many books incorporating athletics and the Christian life, and is founder and president of The Winning Run Foundation, an organization that publishes athletic-related devotional materials. Even though our paths only crossed for a short time, it was certainly not by accident.

After just one semester, however, I transferred to Eastern Kentucky to play for Coach Jim Ward. That's where I had wanted to play after high school, but did not have the chance. Like Coach Johnson at Trevecca, Coach Ward was a fine Christian man. Having mentors like that in my life has helped mold me as a person. It is important to seek out positive role models. Doing so will reward you a hundred times over. I will never forget Coach Ward and Coach Johnson, and I often think about those days. One of the many things I learned from Coach Ward was to be patient and never overreact to a situation. Any time something big came up, Coach Ward would absorb all of the information he could, then step back and evaluate it before making any rash decisions. It's a sound process for decision-making that I try to incorporate into my life.

I remember too that Coach Ward loved eating at Shoney's restaurants. Every time we would play on the road, our itinerary would include a Shoney's meal. I remember one particular time when one of our players, our shortstop, was in the restroom and sitting in a stall inside a Shoney's one day. If you have ever eaten the Shoney's breakfast bar, you can understand how quickly it can affect your bowels. A bunch of us guys were in the restroom, too, cutting up and carrying on. Then Coach Ward walked in and everything quieted down a bit, except for our shortstop, who was in the stall and didn't realize that coach was in the room. Robbie says from the stall, "If I have eaten at Shoney's once, I've eaten there a thousand times . . . blah, blah, blah," and he threw in some expletives to boot. Coach Ward washed his hands and left the room without ever saying a word. The next team meeting, as we were going over our itinerary for the follow day's away game, Coach Ward said, "We will board the bus as 6 a.m. and stop at Shoney's for breakfast, if that's okay with you Robbie McCune?"

11

I have never forgotten the lessons I learned from my coaches, especially Coach Johnson and Coach Ward. In fact, right after my son passed away, I called them. We prayed over the phone and talked about dealing with grief. Their influence is squarely on me to this day.

My first season at Eastern, I had a decent year, you might say, and finished third in batting in the Ohio Valley Conference. I probably would never have gotten to play in the first place, but the starting third baseman Jerry Shane got hurt, giving me a chance to play every day. My junior season at EKU was pretty good, but it turned into a nightmare the next spring when I couldn't hit anything. During the offseason, my hitting coach left and my favorite aluminum bat disappeared. It was old and getting flat on one side. They probably threw it away, but I had hit .340 with it the season before. Partly due to those issues, it didn't take long for my slump to turn to wood—pine wood that is. I was benched and spent nearly a half season riding the pine. That was a difficult period for me as I wasn't accustomed to watching the action. However, it taught me a great lesson and has made me a better coach and teacher. It has helped me to understand what those kids feel like who workout with the team every day, but seldom get on the field. I respect them for their tenacity and heart, for their will and perseverance. It is much more difficult to be second string. It takes character, and it builds character when you are humble enough to wear the colors for the love of the game or the pride in your teammates.

After graduation from Eastern, Shannon and I married on August 24, 1991 at Marion Baptist Church in our hometown. Within days, I was off to Fort Benning, Georgia, for basic training. If you want advice from everyone, just get married and join the U.S. Army in the same month. There were some people who questioned my sensibility about getting a college degree, then going into the army as an enlisted infantry man. We all need to base our decisions on what we are led to do, not what people think we should do.

Shannon, our dog and I arrived in Fort Drum in January of 1992. It is cold and the snow is deep in upstate New York in the dead of winter. Drum is just east of Interstate 81 right between Lake Ontario and the Adirondacks. When we hit the ground in New York, it was forty degrees below zero and the snow was hip deep, or that's the way I remember it. We stayed in some Gomer Pyle-type barracks for the first couple weeks, and the communal bathroom was down the hall from our room. Shannon got sick the first week we were there. She still describes it as the sickest she's ever been in her life. This helped to set her attitude about being a military spouse and living in upstate New York. Why didn't I take her to Hawaii? Life might have been different.

It just got better, too. Shannon was cooking spaghetti and toasting bread one night and set off the fire alarms in the barracks. Before we knew it there were fire trucks out front and firemen running through the building. Shannon was running around trying to tell them that it was just some bread she'd burned, but everyone was panicking.

My military career was not off to an auspicious start.

We soon settled into military life, and it turned out to be among the most rewarding years of my life. As a young couple living on our own, it was a great way for me and Shannon to start out. The first year I was gone a large amount of the time. When our unit was not in the field training, I was in some type of school. The most challenging school by far was Ranger school. On October of 1992, I entered Ranger school at Fort Benning, Georgia. Since I would be driving to Fort Benning from New York, I was allowed to have a couple of days at home before having to report. While at home, my uncle was in a car wreck and was killed. This made the trip to Fort Benning very tough. After completing Ranger school, I was able to sneak my way into Airborne school before returning back to Fort Drum. About two weeks later, I was off on the first of two real world missions on which I would get the privilege to serve.

Probably the best known of those missions was the one in eastern Africa in 1993, which has been branded by popular culture as Black Hawk Down because of a book about the incident. I was assigned to 10th Mountain Division, which was sent to the nation of Somalia to provide safety to those delivering humanitarian aid to the country. There was no real government in the country, and no police or army to protect its own people or the United Nations personnel trying to help.

The U.N. Security Council had authorized UNOSOM II, a declaration aimed at creating a secure environment throughout the country with hopes of achieving national reconciliation. The ultimate objective was to create a democratic state. What we saw was a terribly war-torn country. It is really sad to see people in those types of circumstances with little hope and few chances of improving their situation. I don't remember seeing a building anywhere in the country that didn't have at least one bullet hole in it. The place was ravaged by civil war. Part of our mission was disarming the general population. The problem with doing that was that it left many families vulnerable. Removing their arms—their only source of protection in a country void of government or police protection—was a dilemma. It was difficult to do, but our mission was removing all of the guns. The normal person on the street was glad we were there because it gave them some feeling of safety. One day while we were at our complex, a little boy walked up to me and handed me a World War II era Chinese hand grenade. I was astounded and a bit frightened at first. I think the young fellow sensed that I didn't want the grenade either. I took it, though, and disposed of it properly. This scenario was played out quite often in different ways. Living in the states, it is hard to fathom our children ever living like that.

The battle, which inspired the 1999 book *Black Hawk Down* by Mark Bowden, was originally known as the Battle of Mogadishu or the Battle of the Black Sea. The locals called it the "Day of the Rangers." The battle was fought Oct. 3-4 against militants loyal to warlord Mohamed Farrah Aidid in the streets of the city around a downed military helicopter. I was in the 10th Mountain Division, which provided support in that battle, but my unit had left the country about six weeks before that happened.

While I was serving in East Africa, Shannon was home in Kentucky substitute teaching; and she was pregnant with our first child.

While it was tough on our budding family, my military service is something I am very proud of. It is customary to thank our military men and women for their service, and we should definitely do that. But for me, serving my country was an honor. It gave me an opportunity to do something with real meaning. I found a great deal of self-gratification in serving in the military; and I would do it all over again, if given the opportunity. There is no greater honor than defending others who are unable to defend themselves.

The only thing about serving in the Army is that you don't get much time off, no matter what's happening in your life. Uncle Sam's business comes ahead of everything else; so, when I got a few days leave in April 1993, I hustled back to Kentucky where Shannon was just about ready to give birth. God works kind of like Uncle Sam because his timetable is the one we have to live by. We wanted so badly for Shannon to deliver Jessi while I was on leave that we tried everything in the book to induce her labor. Whatever old wife's tale someone told us, we tried. We walked and rode on a bumpy four-wheeler. Shannon ate things that people said would help promote her having the baby. We were down to only a couple days when Shannon finally went into labor. Being there for the birth of my first child was amazing. Life is such a precious thing and to watch a new one enter into this world surrounded by a loving and caring family is captivating, and even more so when it's yours.

Shannon stayed in Kentucky and I reported back to Fort Drum. About two weeks later, my parents brought her and newborn Jessi to New York. Having the family together was wonderful, but it wasn't going to last very long.

Shannon and the baby went back to Kentucky and Shannon secured a full-time job teaching in the school district where we both had graduated. It is the only high school in the county of about 9,000 people. There are only about 400 students in ninth through 12th grade. Basketball is her passion, and she started coaching the girls' varsity team. That meant she was responsible for every female basketball league from varsity down. Putting together youth leagues

15

and middle school teams, finding coaches and helping raise money for the booster clubs was all part of the contract. It was a full-time job on top of teaching that paid an extra $5,000 a year, but she loves it and is still doing the same job today.

Over the next year and half, my unit was sent to Panama for training and we were deployed to Haiti for two months during 1994 for a peacekeeping operation. We were there to promote democracy and provide humanitarian relief. I was discharged from the U.S. Army on Christmas Eve 1994 after serving three years and three months and achieving the rank of E5, sergeant. With one of the most rewarding periods of my life behind me, I went home to the small western Kentucky town where I was raised. Full of great ideas and energy, I was ready to tackle anything. Teaching school at my alma mater was the plan, but it would have to wait. There were no jobs in physical education, so I took a position as director of the migrant program. I worked with children and families who had recently moved into the school district. We tried to facilitate a great number of needs, and I learned quickly that families in rural western Kentucky were struggling to survive. It was different, but in many ways somewhat similar to my missions in the military. Again, I was providing humanitarian aid. This time, it was in my backyard. My military experience and my work with the migrant program showed me many things, among them, that there is no real correlation between money or living conditions and happiness. Some of the jolliest, friendliest, happiest people on this earth have virtually nothing but their smiles. In third world countries, the children did not know how unfortunate they were. And as I grow older, I have started to think whether they are really unfortunate, or are they lucky not to have to deal with the pressures of running the rat race. They have nothing better with which to compare their lives. In our own society, less fortunate children do not recognize their plight until they reach late elementary or early middle school age. That's when they start looking around and realizing that they don't wear the same clothes or have the same opportunities as other children. It is a terribly difficult time for those kids. Some overcome their environment, but most perpetuate the lifestyle. Every child should have the same opportunities to be successful. In our country, there is at least some glimpse of hope for even the poorest boy or girl. In other places around the globe, that isn't true.

Within a year after I had returned home from the Army, our son Jake was born at the hospital in Crittenden County, Kentucky on September 5, 1995. He was born with a touch of jaundice, and we had to take him to Evansville, Indiana, where he stayed under a light at another hospital for a few days. I always joked around, telling Jake that his sister was born at Fort Campbell, Kentucky on the military base and it cost me just $18. His birth was substantially more. As time has gone by, the sister's expenses have indeed caught up.

Reflecting on our life in rural western Kentucky, I realize that we are somewhat isolated from many things that go on in this sometimes crazy and sometimes brutal world. That's why I have never shied away from exposing my children, and even my students, to worldly events. The church is also good at teaching perspective to boys and girls who live in a normal home with parents who love and care for them. When my son was about 10, he and I and some others from our church went on a mission trip to Omaha, Nebraska. We spent time in a Sudanese community; most were refugees from their own country. It was a great opportunity for the kids and adults in our church to see how others are affected by things beyond their control and how difficult life can be. We also did some work on American Indian reservations in Nebraska. Children living in good Christian homes are very lucky. We must remember, however, that not all children are as fortunate. We have to reach out to those with every ounce of our energy. From our time in the Indian villages, we learned that it does indeed take the whole tribe to raise a child. I was proud that my family was in the small, western Kentucky county where Shannon and I had grown up. We would come to know how important family and friends are, and how important they are on our lives and the lives of our children. The love my community showed when Jake died was enormous. Because of that, I will continue, for the rest of my time on this Earth, to contribute something to my community. I may retire from my job, but I will continue devoting my time and resources to a community for which I have undying compassion and appreciation.

CHAPTER 4

Follow Me Parenting

Down every path in life, there is a need to follow. Military leaders ask their soldiers to follow their lead. Coaches ask players to follow their game plan and run the plays that will net the best results. Likewise, teachers are leaders for their students, directing them through formulas and through processes that will help them arrive at the correct answer.

As parents, we must lead by example—mentally, physically, socially and spiritually.

One thing Shannon and I tried to teach our children, Jessi and Jake, was to lead by example, whether in the classroom, on the court, in the rodeo arena or in a social setting.

It is easy to become a "do as I say" parent. However, it is more difficult to become a "follow me" parent. Our children watch everything we do. They emulate us, good and bad.

As a teacher and coach, I see kids who are in trouble at school. Many times parents tell the kids to do one thing, while they are doing the exact opposite. Parents, who tell their children to be disciplined, need to practice the same discipline in their own lives.

Jesus encouraged his followers to "pick up your cross and follow me." Likewise, the U.S. Army infantry motto is "follow me." There's a U.S. Army memorial called Follow Me at Fort Benning, Georgia. Two soldiers created it in 1959. The statue depicts a 1950s-era infantry soldier charging forward and gesturing for others to follow. Soldiers at Infantry School call the statue "Iron Mike." A few years ago, a new bronze version was made and the original statue was moved to the National Infantry Museum in South Columbus, Georgia just outside Fort Benning.

Unless you're a military type person, you probably don't get much from the statue of a guy carrying a carbine with a fixed bayonet and grenades hanging off his fatigues. But for those who understand the creed, it's a moving piece.

Many people say today's younger generation has problems. I say today's generation is a reflection of the adults in society. All of us would agree that the breakdown of the traditional family in American society is a grave concern. One of the things we try to do is eat together. When my children were young, and even as they grew older, Shannon and I would make them sit at the dinner table with us. They had a misguided interpretation that they were being punished. They would pout for a while, because they could not see the TV, but soon we'd all be engaged in conversation and the kids would talk their heads off. Jake always started what he was going to say like this: "Mom, remember when . . . ."

In the freshmen health classes that I teach, we discuss family issues with the students. Often students discuss their family situations, and some of the stories they can tell are quite interesting. One of the stories I like to retell was shared by a student when we were studying the disadvantages of credit and rent to own. Well, a young man in the back raised his hand. I knew it was going to be good when I called on him. Let's call him little Johnny. Well, little Johnny commenced to tell the story of how his family had bought a poodle at the pet store. Johnny told us that they didn't make the payments and the pet store came and repossessed their $300 star poodle. On a more serious note, an informal survey in freshmen classes will show almost twenty percent of the family homes in our county include a mother with children and no father present. That's not a large number compared to many other places in the country, but it still amounts to nearly one in five children living in a single-parent home. And in most of my classes you will find that only about 40% of the students come from a traditional home situation. Very seldom, when they discuss their family situation, do students say that divorce has led to a better environment for them.

My children have always been quick to tell me when I haven't lived up to the standards Shannon and I set out for the family. They're always quick to let me know if I failed to practice what I preach. Having a daughter has made me realize that her young eyes—and her boyfriends—are watching the way I treat my wife. It should be our desire as fathers to treat our wives in a way that will have a positive influence on young men. Where else are they going to learn how to treat women? Certainly not from television, unless they watch reruns of Leave it to Beaver. Teens are usually not really good at listening to adults, but they are great at imitating them. Young boys, especially, are pretty good at doing what dad says; but as they age, they tend to do as dad does. For this reason, we should model appropriate behavior, both to adults and youth.

Parents are leaders, so I asked several teachers in our school system to write down what they think makes a good leader. Some of them had in their mind what they should be doing, and some were thinking what they would want their boss to do. But the quotes of what a leader should do are great examples of how we in many ways should parent our children.

- Real leaders motivate, inspire and lead by example.
- Real leaders set standards.
- Real leaders can admit they made a mistake.
- Real leaders make other leaders.
- Real leaders remember their roots.
- Real leaders duplicate themselves.
- Real leaders give and earn respect.
- Real leaders thrive under pressure, not fold.

- Real leaders aren't afraid to be different, but seek out what is best for their organization (students) even if it's never been done before.
- Real leaders live a life of character and integrity.
- Real leaders have willing followers.
- Real leaders lead by example, not by words.
- Real leaders lead by example, using only what they have, such as their mind, body, heart and soul.
- Real leaders are the people you go to when you have a problem. If they don't have an answer, they will look/work until they do.
- Real leaders often take the path less traveled.
- Real leaders listen before they react/respond.
- Real leaders are motivators, inspiring others to want to do their best.
- Real leaders motivate and inspire.
- Real leaders plan ahead.
- Real leaders always do what is right even if it is not the most popular decision.
- Real leaders can see the big picture and have long term visions.
- Real leaders anticipate problems.
- Real leaders develop other leaders in their organization.
- Real leaders surround themselves with weaknesses to make everyone stronger.
- Real leaders encourage not discourage.
- Real leaders do not ask of others what they themselves would not do.
- Real leaders make everyone around them better.
- Real leaders bring people together.

The winter of 2009 was very difficult for Kentucky. A major ice and snow storm hit the last couple of days in January, knocking out utilities for nearly everyone. We went without water for a couple of days and had no electricity for about a week. Some people in the county went many more days without power.

For many, it was a very tough time. It taught us about being prepared for an emergency. It is very important for us to teach ourselves to be independent.

The inspiration of this story comes from three cats that live at my house.

The old cat is Whitey. She is a hunter. Whitey has had many kittens which my family loves. Her kittens are raised tough. She will give birth in the most remote places like in the weeds or woods around the house. She will hide them until they are old enough to come to the house.

Whitey's kittens become hunters just like their mother, and then they move on to another location. They return from time to time to eat from the dog food bowl, but mostly they are survivors like their mother—they live off the land.

We also have two other cats that were dropped off here by friends of ours in hopes that they would be barn cats and hunt mice like Whitey. However, my wife's uncle Jerry loves cats and was here every day helping us work on our house. Jerry would feed the cats every day. He thought he was helping the cats by taking care of them. But what he did was take away their hunting skills. Now, they have become totally reliant on us to feed them. Sadly, they are almost too lazy to walk to the barn to the dog food bowl.

I wonder how God views us and the way we raise our children. I was taught as an Army Ranger to adapt, adjust and overcome. I was taught that it is okay to be miserable for short periods of time in order to reach a higher goal.

We, as Americans, have quickly become dependent on our comforts and conveniences. We have trouble sacrificing physically, financially or spiritually to meet a goal.

Like the cats, what are we teaching our children? Are we teaching them to work, hunt and sacrifice to reach our goals? Or are we teaching them to be like the bigger cats that stand on the porch until someone feeds them?

We also must be willing to let our children try different things, even if it means failure, because those are the best teaching moments. We have always encouraged our children to try; and if they make mistakes, it is okay, if you learn from them.

What have you sacrificed to become spiritually right? Have you let your children go hungry to become hunters?

As parents, when we look at our own children we see that they are a lot like us. They look like us, talk like us, walk like us and think like us in many respects. As we are raising our children, it is important that we take a long hard look at ourselves. We must be sure we are worthy of reflection, living by the light of God so that our children will do the same, not because we ask them to, but because they see us doing it.

Because our children are a reflection of us, it is important that we show them hard work every day whether being a good father, a good husband, a good business man, a good teacher, a good coach or whatever. It is not easy raising children. The more we put into them, and the more we work to be good parents, the greater the rewards for both parent and child.

Being a good parent requires many things. Among the most important tools are good health, patience, and spiritual and physical strength. My military training helped a great deal with introspection and self evaluation because it taught me that making good decisions requires self-discipline. In Ranger school, we would train at night, many times after being awake for hours and hours and deprived of food. I remember one cold night while we were on a mountain in Georgia. Everyone in my Ranger training squad was tired and hungry. A soldier friend had figured out to stay warm using his poncho as a mini tent. He draped the rain gear over his head and lit a can of Sterno. This can is fuel made from denatured and jellied alcohol. In the military, we used it to heat up MREs (meals ready to eat). In restaurants it is used to heat food on buffet tables. Once lit, it is like a small campfire in a can. Well, this guy had it between his legs and I guess he fell asleep. Next thing I know, he's on fire. I ran over and patted him out and was laughing because he'd burned a big hole in his poncho. Come to find out, he'd borrowed—for a lack of a stronger word—my poncho. So I went around the rest of the mission with a drafty poncho.

I also learned another very valuable lesson in ranger training. Each solider gets the chance to be in charge of patrols. If your patrol goes well, you pass; if not, you fail. One patrol I was in charge of went pretty well. I was very busy running around taking care of every thing, except I forgot one thing. I forgot to clean my own weapon. I was so busy making sure everything was going well for everyone else I forgot to take care of myself. When I was evaluated, I got a bad score. The moral to this story is that as parents, it's important to keep ourselves mentally and physically sharp for the rigors of parenting. I let myself become sidetracked in various ways on that mountain training mission and lost sight of my overall objective and the details that went into meeting those objectives. As parents, we can't afford to let that happen. Distractions can cause us to take our eye off the ball. Being able to focus on the mission we have as parents requires us to be spiritually and physically fit. Our minds and bodies need to be at peak performance. We can become so wrapped up in our jobs, our social activities, or simply making sure our children have the things they want and need that we forget to keep ourselves fit for the job. Exercise and spiritual introspection will help us be prepared and stay focused when distractions mount around us.

Our challenge is to be a follow me parent. Take time to step back and see the big picture. And don't forget to clean your own weapon. You must keep yourself physically strong, morally straight, and spiritually ready to be the best follow me parent you can be.

CHAPTER 5

Sports on Sunday

What should a follow me parent do about sports on Sunday? As a Christian parent of a student-athlete, one of the toughest decisions you will face is to what extent you will let your child participate in sports that compete on Sunday. I have faced this decision with both of my children. I struggle with this issue so I asked for advice from some Christian friends. I will address the question and share with you some of the wisdom that I have gained from God's word and Christian friends. There are two big questions and one reality that have to be addressed in order to reach your conclusion about what is right for you and your family concerning Sunday sports. After you ask these questions, stop and listen to what God has to tell you. Listen to His plan for you and your children.

Are you beginning with the end in mind? What do you plan to accomplish by having your child play sports on Sunday? Is this league going to help them become the next Alex Rodriguez? Will your child miss out and fall behind their peers athletically? I have a good friend who travels all over the country to take his son to baseball tryouts, camps, and combines in hopes of obtaining a college scholarship. He is a single parent who is a great father and has raised a wonderful young man. The truth is that he has probably spent enough money traveling to pay for his son's first two years of college without a hint of scholarship. They have spent countless hours together, which does not come with a price tag. I doubt they would have spent nearly as much time together if it were not for their travels for baseball. This young man is a really good player and will probably end up playing for a small Division 1 college. The question is: When it is over, then what? Have you begun the season with the end in mind?

Have you done every thing you can to prepare them to not only play the game well but to meet God? If your child kisses his mother tomorrow night, tells her he loves her, falls off to sleep and slips away into eternity like my son Jake did, are you certain that you have prepared him to meet God? My brother-in-law is a very close friend. He is a fine Christian man. He loves his family and has two young boys, who he has in church on most Sundays. On occasion, he will take the older son hunting on Sunday morning instead of going to church. It is an opportunity to bond with his son. At times, other family members go along—sometimes his brother and maybe his father, too. What a great time this must be for the men of the family, out hunting together, enjoying God's natural world. These are times that will be remembered for a lifetime and something every man would long to do with their father, brother, and son. The question that must be answered at the end of the day is: Have you done everything you can to prepare your children to meet God?

Fact is that all of our children are going to die. If you have found a way around this deal of dying, please let me know because we could sell the plan and make lots of money, which we would give to the church, of course. Truth is that I thank God every day that I have a Christian wife with godly wisdom who helps raise our children with the end in mind. Shannon has even found a way to communicate with our 16-year-old daughter. She writes in a journal most every evening and leaves it on Jessi's night stand after she prays with her. An analogy I often use is that our lives are like those cell phone minutes you can buy at Wal-Mart. That is something most youngsters can understand really well. We all would like unlimited minutes with free texting. In reality, we all are operating on a certain number of minutes on this Earth. There are no rollover minutes in life. When they're gone, they're gone. We will be judged on what we have done with those minutes. We must ask ourselves this: What are we doing with our allotted minutes? Are we using them as God would have us to use them? My goal is to get full use out of each one of those minutes; to use them in the way that God would have me to use them. I fail at that goal every day, but that is still my goal. Lord willing—and if I keep my health—I am never going to retire because I want to be used up when I die. Longtime Florida State football coach Bobby Bowden said, "There is only one big event after retirement, and I am not looking forward to it." How will you use the minutes you have? Will you watch more television, work extra at the office, play with your children, visit with your wife, read your Bible, go on a mission trip, or just relax at home? I challenge you to consult God to see if He has a plan for your minutes. Who knows, He might give you some rollover time if you are living by His plan not just yours.

Back to the original discussion about sports on Sundays, I have faced this Sunday and sports issue with my own children over the years. When Jessi was about nine years old, she got into junior rodeo. I made the mistake of letting her go one night with a friend of mine named Jamie Brown. Jamie took Jessi and his daughter, Bailey, to a little county rodeo. To hear the story, Jessi must have made the luckiest over the shoulder throw known to the rodeo world. Jamie swears that Roy Cooper could not have done it any better, and Jessi was hooked on rodeo. I am sure as parents you have entered into deals like this in which you really didn't know what you were getting into until it was too late. The most important thing in the rodeo world is the horse. Good ones are very expensive. What a lot of people do is buy one that has potential and let their children, or someone they know, train the horse.

This is where it gets good. I bought a horse from some horse trading friends of ours for $1,000 which is pretty cheap for a good mount. I loved this horse and we named her Cheyenne. There was just one problem with Cheyenne, she was half quarter horse and half thoroughbred—very fast but she liked to buck from time to time. On a scale of one to 10, she gets a 10 for bucking. Sometimes we thought she should be in the saddle bronc event instead of barrel

29

racing. One day I decided that we had too many horses, so I sold Cheyenne to a young man that I knew. I told him I really liked the horse and if he decided he didn't want her anymore to just give me a call and I would take her back. I don't think I ever cashed the check. The young man's name is David. He called me about a week after buying the horse and said, "Coach, I hate to call you, but this horse . . . I had been riding her all day. Me and my girlfriend were riding her double and she bucked us off and ran to Sheridan." Sheridan is a small town near where they were riding. I told David to just bring her home and I would give him his money back.

I was kind of glad to see her come back. One day, Jessi and I were going for a ride around the farm. I was riding Cheyenne, and Jessi was riding some other horse we had. She was about 10 years old at this point and she looked over at me and said, "Can I ride Cheyenne?" What a moment of truth. I agreed to let her try, thinking the whole time that her mom would kill me if she knew. That was about eight years ago. I can look out of my front window today and still see Cheyenne eating on a bale of hay. After two concussions—thanks to being bucked off, three all-around state championships, and five trips to the Wrangler National Rodeo Finals in New Mexico, here we are today in Jessi's junior season of high school rodeo. We have attended numerous cowboy church services and missed many Sundays at our home church. There are times, I admit, that my family still struggles with the same questions about Sunday sports and whether we're doing the right thing for our children.

With Jake, we faced the same dilemma. When he was about 10 years old some of the parents decided to organize a travel baseball team instead of playing in our community's summer league. Of course, the main concern that all of us had was how much we would miss going to our church on Sundays. The first year it wasn't a problem because we often got beat and knocked out of weekend tournaments before the final rounds. That meant we were back home for Sunday church. As the team got better things started to change. We did end up missing some Sunday services during the summer. Jake also wanted to be like his sister, and he too participated in junior rodeo, which was not a problem because we were going to be there for the weekend anyway. Jake had also made it to the Wrangler Junior Rodeo Association finals. He died one week before we were to leave for the rodeo. Jake and I were going to go to the junior finals and then come back while his sister Jessi and Shannon were going to stay in Farmington, New Mexico, for the high school finals, for which Jessi had qualified. As I reflect on the whole picture, I have decided that we have done the right thing with our children in regards to how we spent our time preparing them for both their competitions and their afterlives.

There were over 2,000 people who visited the funeral services for Jake. The calls and cards came from literally all over the country, and the love shown by friends and strangers alike was overwhelming. Jake's life touched so many people in such a short amount of time. The time we spend on this earth is not the question. It's what we do with the minutes we're here. Graveyards are full of people who had lots of unused minutes. Jake did more living and touched more lives in 12 years than many do in a much longer lifetime. Not only was he a Christian, but he was able to share his Christian values and change the lives of many people, young and old, that he came into contact with through sports, rodeo, and life in general.

My friend Greg Hollamon, who is the best math teacher I know, a great Christian dad and a Bible scholar, has helped me see the light in regard to Sunday and sports. He has helped me sum it up in the following manner. Sunday, being the first day of the week, is the day of worship as instructed by God in the New Testament. Restrictions placed on the Sabbath (Saturday) in the Old Testament are not placed on Sunday. The focus on Sunday is supposed to be on worshiping God, but time and length are not specified. In fact, because many early Christians worked on Sunday, they had to meet at night, while others worshipped throughout the day.

The question is, do sports prevent us from worshiping, or do they take priority over God? Sports have become a religion in our society where people worship their team or particular sport over God. That is where we go wrong. Also, I have been to a few professional ball games and found that the atmosphere was far from family friendly, or what God might approve.

We should work on making God more prevalent in whatever we're doing every day of the week. One thing I might suggest is that if you play sports on the weekends, and cannot attend your regular church service, find ways to work God into the day. My friend and co-writer of this book, Chris Evans, remembers Dave Concepcion, an all-star shortstop, who played baseball for the Cincinnati Reds during their storied years in the 1970s. Concepcion was a devout Catholic, who crossed himself every time he walked to the plate. We could honor God in similar fashion by remembering him and all that he has done for us each time we put on our mitt, or each time we field a ground ball. One thing we would do with our travel team was have one of the dads do a Sunday devotional. It's easy to find a way to honor our Lord, but it's even easier to forget to do it. Don't fall into that trap. Take time and make time for Him, no matter where you are—between the lines or on the pew. If you lead a purpose driven life, God has put you in your situation for a reason, so glorify him wherever you are.

In summation, as with all things, the attitude with which we approach God is the most important. We must follow the instructions that God has given us. That should dictate activities on Sunday, as well as our entire lives. If any activity interferes with the worship of God on Sunday, then it should be considered wrong. I know that there are many Christian people who can't be in the church every Sunday. But for most of us, when we are not in church on Sunday, there is something inside us that longs for or tells us that we are missing something very important in our lives.

This team photograph was at a youth baseball tournament where Jake's club won second place. Some of the kids were happy, some were upset with the finish. They wanted to win the championship. Pictured are (from left) Keagan Gillette, Taylor Champion, Travis Gilbert, Landon Young, Blake Shuecraft, Aaron Owen, (second row) coach Kevin Young, coach Brad Gilbert, Brenden Phillips, Paxton James, Colby Watson, Tommy Baker with Logan Young on shoulders, Devin Belt, Jake Hodge and coach Denis Hodge.

Jake's first birthday was attended by his family. Pictured are (front from left) Pat Collins, Jake, Chris Hodge, (back) Dadie Belt, Anna Collins, Tony Collins, Aileen Hodge, Keith Hodge, Emma Curnel, George Curnel and Hayden Hodge.

On vacation beside the ocean are (from left) Shannon holding the Hodges' youngest child, Jordyn, Denis, Jessi and Jessi's boyfriend Brandon Sigler.

The author, Denis Hodge, goes over a play with the youth basketball team he coached in 2006. Jake is No. 11.

Here are Jake and Jessi (in the middle) on a pony cart Jessi bought with own money. The other girls in the photograph are their cousins, Maggie and Mauri Collins. The horse's name is Gracie.

This photograph was taken at the youth football banquet when the boys were in elementary school. Pictured are (from left) Travis Gilbert, Brenden Phillips, Aaron Own, Jake and Taylor Champion.

Here is Jake at age 5 with family friend Payton Croft and a catfish they caught at Jimmy Croft's pond.

Jake stopped to salute his teammates after hitting a grand slam in the last baseball game he played in June 2008.

Jake played junior pro football in elementary school.

Jake was an outstanding young point guard.

The author, Denis Hodge, coached his son Jake almost every season. Their bond remains unbroken.

CHAPTER 6

Gaining Victory in Defeat

Some of the best teaching moments in life come from losses. In my life this has been especially true. I consider myself a bit of a slow learner, and that can sometimes be a disadvantage. However, it can come in handy. For instance, if you are a bull rider you might need to have a short memory, so you can't remember what happened the last time you rode. Pain itself can be a great teacher, if used properly. Pain can teach us not to touch something; or in sports, it can convince us to use the proper technique, so we don't feel so much pain.

We use loss and pain in the education of our children, and God uses those teaching tools, too. In my life, I have learned more from my losses than I ever have from my victories. At times, all I can remember are the losses, and I wonder if there have ever been any victories. For me, sports and competition have provided many of life's lessons. I try to pass along to children those experiences so that they may benefit from them. If we indeed learn from our experiences and do not repeat mistakes, we will lead more rewarding lives. From that, we can leave a lasting positive legacy. One of the best things you can teach children is how to recover from a big loss, whether it's sports-related or otherwise. You might have an automobile accident and lose your car, a good friend might move to another state, or you might work hard but still fail a test in school.

Lou Holtz says successful people are not ones who don't get knocked down. He says truly successful people are the ones who keep getting up.

One example of me being a slow learner happened in the summer I played American Legion baseball in Paducah, Kentucky with a bunch of guys that were really super athletes. I hit second in the lineup. Junior Shumpert was leadoff and Terry Shumpert, a future big leaguer, hit third. I started thinking I was pretty good. I was too intellectually slow to realize that all I had to hit were fastballs. Junior always got on base and stole second, and many times third base, too. Pitchers were always paying attention to him and not worried about me. On deck was Terry Shumpert, who went on to play at the University of Kentucky, then later replaced Hall of Famer Frank White as second baseman of the Kansas City Royals. He played for other major league teams and then became a coach. Most pitchers didn't even know I was in the lineup. I could have probably just run to first base, and they would not have noticed. We won more than 50 games and the state championship that summer, but the thing I remember most was getting beat in the Mid-South Regional in Woodward, Oklahoma. We had Gonzales, Louisiana down and were looking to beat them when the Louisiana club put men on first and second.

Our coach Dr. Frank "Doc" Hideg came out to the mound and talked to our pitcher, Tracy Thompson, who hailed from nearby Ballard County, Kentucky. The conversation went something like this, "Tracy we need to walk this guy," Doc said.

"No, Doc, I think I can get him," Tracy said.

Doc went back to the dugout and asked our statistician—whom we all called affectionately, Joe Baby, what day it was. Joe Baby said, "It is Saturday, Doc."

"I will be back to work on Monday," said Doc, who was a chiropractor by trade and only volunteered to coach the Legion team.

Doc had seen this guy hit on television. His name was Patterson. He had played for Louisiana State University and was the Designated Hitter of the Year in the Southeastern Conference. I can't remember what position I was playing that game, but I do recall watching that ball going out of the lights and into the western Oklahoma desert. I am not sure what moral lesson that tells us, but Tracy should have listened to the old ball coach. If he had, we might have been in the American Legion World Series that summer.

The lesson I draw from this situation is that I should take time to listen to my personal head coach, who is God. Like our pitcher, I admit that I haven't always listened to my coach. If I had, I might have been able to avoid some of the messes I have gotten myself into.

One of the best lessons I ever learned about losing was from Jeff Jackson, a very successful high school basketball coach in western Kentucky during the 1990s. I am sure that to this day, Jeff has had no idea how much his high-class actions have affected my life. He was the high school basketball coach of a small, private school named University Heights Academy in Hopkinsville, Kentucky, which has produced many Division I college basketball players. The team had also won several Class A state basketball championships and a couple of Kentucky Sweet 16 championships, which in Kentucky is an unclassified state championship. For several years, University Heights beat the tar out of our little county high school where I was assistant coach. One year we finally beat them on the way to our first Class A regional title. After we beat them, Jeff came to us and congratulated us. He told us how much we deserved the success and how we had earned the win. The class that Coach Jackson showed in defeat set a great example for me and changed how I handle defeat.

The great thing about sports is there are always winners and losers, and life lessons to be learned. I took the opportunity once to help Jake learn a lesson about handling defeat. Understand that the teacher and student are both pretty sore losers. When Jake was about five years old, I recall a conversation I had with friend and fellow coach, Rob Towery. Our discussion was about whether the desire to win and the hatred of losing are learned from practice and hard work or an inherent trait somehow bred into us. Being the great parent I am, I duly volunteered my son for a case study. We put up a goal at the school gymnasium low enough for Jake to play basketball. I made sure he knew we were going to 10. So we played for a while and he got ahead by one—9 to 8. It was match point, so to speak, and he thought he was going to win. I scored to tie it, then stole the ball from him and scored to win the game. Yeah, I beat the five year old. When he realized he had lost he started to cry and went over on a dark stairwell, sat down and pouted with his arms crossed on his chest.

We—the two coaches and managers of this unscientific study—determined that the sore losing came from his mother. In all honesty, the real lesson I learned was that we have to use these moments to teach. We can't always let our children win. We need to teach them how to handle defeat.

When Jake was about 12, we had a travel basketball team that played at Paducah Athletic Club in western Kentucky. We did very well, but got beat in the championship game of the tournament. This didn't sit well with Jake. He wanted to throw his second place trophy in the nearby Cumberland River. If his mom hadn't been with us on the drive home, I might have let him do it. I later found the trophy in his room broke in half with second place marked out. We don't have to enjoy losing; we just need to understand how to handle it. Trying to shelter children from failure is the wrong answer.

Parents miss out on excellent teaching opportunities in sports when they take the easiest road and simply blame others for failure. It is so easy to blame an official or referee, or even another player or a coach, for a loss. I have been guilty of blaming an official for a loss, and so have most parents of athletes. In life, we must learn to control what we can control and to get better by learning from our mistakes. Blaming others is an excuse that will prevent you or your children from getting better.

When Jake died, it was my greatest loss. I felt like it was the end. God had my full attention and he told me it wasn't the end. Instead, He told me it was time to show the faith that I have talked about. It was time to practice what I had been preaching. Like Jeff Jackson had taught me in basketball, it was time to glorify God in my lowest hour.

I was to speak at the funeral, start a scholarship program to raise $100,000 and write a book to help parents raise children to leave a lasting legacy. God willing, I will see all three of these directives finished. I have tried to personally deal with the loss of my son, in some respects, the way people deal with losing a big game. I have been able to use Jake's life and death as a teaching lesson. Most of all, I have tried to use this personal tragedy as an opportunity to share my faith and witness to others. Our only true job on this earth is to glorify God. Our family and many friends have been inspired by Jake's life. It has prompted personal introspection and has pushed us toward helping others in God's name. Through our outreach program and the All Pro Dads chapters we started in our hometown, our mission is to praise God for all that He has done for us and to share our blueprint for living a life that is acceptable to Him. It brings me joy and great peace to think that the life of my son has inspired others to become closer to Christ and to do so much good for their fellow man.

Even with this purpose and drive that Jake's life and death have inspired, there remains a great void. Losing a child leaves a hole in your soul that nothing can fill. It feels like a blob of concrete you carry around in your stomach, but it's really an empty feeling. The pain is never ceasing. As I write, it has been almost two years since his death. I still find myself in tears. But that's okay because I have always told my children that crying is like throwing up. You really don't want to do it, but after it is over you feel a little better for a while.

CHAPTER 7

The Trap

My wife and I generally expect good from humanity. As Christians, we should look for Godliness in all things, but it's also prudent to be on guard because the devil is often in the detail. Something that seems too good to be true usually is, whether it's a free vacation or no-charge minutes on our cell phones.

One such story I recall began with a trip to Florida for a family vacation in 1997. Shannon and I and our two children, Jessi and Jake, went south for some fun and sun.

I am embarrassed to say that I fell into a trap during this family excursion. We were having a great vacation and a wonderful time in Florida. We took the children to the beach. Jake was two years old and Jessi was four. They had a blast, and it was the best of times for the whole family.

My parents went along too, and they kept the kids while Shannon and I went on a short cruise to the Bahamas. The entire trip was all part of a diabolical trap set for our young, unsuspecting family. By the time it had sprung, we were caught like mice.

We had received an offer of a greatly-discounted vacation. All we had to do was sit through a 90-minute presentation by the vacation sponsor. It was a timeshare investment opportunity, according to the colorful marketing material. Bait, as I will now refer to it.

As it turns out, for a reasonable sum, you get a deed to a piece of vacation property for one week every year. You and the whole family can take a vacation annually. The only recurring cost is a small maintenance fee. For an additional fee, you can even change the location of your vacation. Go out West if you want or go skiing in the mountains. It's a near-perfect opportunity, or so we were led to believe.

These battle-tested timeshare salespeople are hard-core veterans, who have set many successful ambushes. They have really racked up the body count of successful buyers. When they present the product, it sounds like paradise, something you can enjoy for years to come. You might even want to pass it along to your offspring one day. The possibilities are endless, right?

The truth is that you might pass it on to your children, but not as an investment—a huge burden. The contract is so extensive that it takes hours to read and digest. The language in these contracts takes a team of lawyers to interpret. In the end, you are not in control of the cost; and the association you've joined can assess fees at its sole discretion. In the initial excitement of becoming proud owners of a vacation home in sunny Florida, you fail to see the long term burden that this trap can create.

Many things that this life has to offer can end up similarly to what my family calls the time-share trap. We don't have to be rigid and vigilant all of the time; but we should certainly be on the lookout for situations that have immediate appeal along with undetermined, long term ramifications. Those types of situations occur often throughout our lives. The way we handle them can have consequences both good and bad.

Something as simple as putting a computer or television in your child's bedroom can have lasting effects. A computer is not a bad thing if used properly and with some oversight. However, without the proper training and safeguards, a computer can prohibit family time and allow people from all over the world to access your child's bedroom via the Internet.

Life's traps come in many different forms. Some of the most common include addictions to things like drugs, alcohol and sex. Each begins with great pleasure and seems very innocent. It's true that sin will take you further than you wanted to go and keep you longer than you ever intended to stay. Just like a time-share passed along with your estate, decisions last a lifetime. Your decisions are passed on as a legacy for your children and grandchildren. I want to leave a legacy that will help my children and grandchildren be mentally and spiritually strong. I want them to buy into my belief of the importance of education, physical fitness, moral character, financial prudence, and Christian values. Those are lasting values that never become burdens.

As a coach and teacher I have witnessed legacies of all shapes and sizes being passed down from generation to generation. It is fascinating to see students come through high school and observe their character. I know many of their parents or grandparents, or both. Not only do they often bear strong physical resemblances to their parents, but many times they possess the same persona. Their values mirror those of their parents. Some greatly value their education, some have strong spiritual values, and others have great manners and integrity. The same is true on the negative side. Parents, who do not put a high value on strong moral character, almost always produce children with similar weaknesses.

Living in a small town, it's easy to know the background of many of the children who pass through the hallways at our school. I wouldn't be sincere if I said that I don't treat some children a particular way because I knew their parent or grandparent. However, I don't mean that to be prejudicial. Let me explain. There is a young man in our school named Ethan. Now, he's a great a kid who is kind to everyone and is loved by students and teachers alike. My relationship with Ethan is not only based on upon my experiences with him, but also with his grandfather, Mr. Easley Hill. Mr. Hill was a farmer

47

for whom I worked as a teenager. Easley Hill always worked hard and expected his hired hands to work hard. He paid us well and showed us a great deal of respect any time my friends and I worked on his farm. Even though that was about 30 years ago, I remember the values he portrayed. I could literally feel the warm vibrations coming from his strength and character. Because I knew the type of man he was, I know that his grandson has some big shoes to fill. I expect Ethan, and others like him, to live up to their lineage, the heritage their families have set for them. These same expectations are also shared by his parents. There are times when those students might feel as though I am being extra tough on them, expecting a little more than I might from the next guy. It's true, and one day I think they will fully understand why. Ethan may not always view this legacy thing such a blessing. But as he continues to mature into a man, everyone around him can see that he too is going to be a man of character, integrity, and spiritual values. He has also earned my respect and has become a very good friend.

For children who have grown up in less than desirable situations, finding the right course can be difficult. I try to empathize with those cases and want desperately for them to understand that good character starts today. That lineage of strong moral forthrightness begins somewhere, and it should begin with them. We should all help these young people to clearly see the many traps that are set for them.

CHAPTER 8

What's Your Give-Up Point?

If you ever watch the Discovery Channel, you might have seen the special on lion hunting. One scene is about the lions hunting a wildebeest. Metaphorically, the wildebeest is like a cross between a Kentucky whitetail deer and a Texas longhorn. You know the story if Discovery Channel is there. The lions sneak up and attack; then they try to cut out a weak cow if possible. The cow will fight for a while, kicking and using her horns to try to hook the lions. Then at some point, you can see the prey slump her shoulders and drop her head.

You have seen it on television and you have seen it in people, how they give up. The question I want you to ask yourself is what is your give-up point and why? Because you are reading this book, the answer is probably, "I will never give up on my children."

Truth is, there is a give-up point for almost everyone, even when it involves their children. I am sure most of us have had a brief moment when we might want to give up on them. Some examples might be when they don't try in school, when they talk back, when they make the same mistakes over and over in sports, or when they turn 16 years old and they are somehow immediately smarter than you. We all know that at 16, you are as smart as you are going to get. The rest is just down hill. I am 41 and continue to get dumber each day, some days are worse than others, if you know what I mean.

What is your give-up point in your marriage, your job, your hobby or your friendships?

The military gives us so much insight on how not to give up. Before I could go to Ranger school, I had to learn what is known as the Ranger Creed. One part of the creed says "Surrender is not a Ranger word. I will never leave a fallen comrade to fall into the hands of the enemy, and under no circumstances will I ever embarrass my country."

That part of the creed has gotten some good Rangers in tight spots over the years because Rangers never leave their buddies, dead or alive. Why will they not surrender or leave their buddies? Simply put, because they have been through the fire before. Rangers train hard and many of them know the hissing sound that a 7.62-millimeter bullet makes as it's piercing the air above their head. I can assure you, it is a sound you will never forget.

While training in the military, one of my commanders quoted a Russian general as saying, "Hard training makes for easy combat." A Naval Seal commander was once quoted as saying, "The more I sweat in training, the less I bleed in combat." There is one common factor in elite troops all over the world, and that is they have a high give-up point. The reason for that high threshold is complex, but the main thing is that they have been through the fire before.

Many people never obtain a high give-up point. I was coaching high school baseball and we got beat in the Class A regional championship game. Both teams had worked very hard to be in that position and neither wanted to give in. It was a classic game. Both pitchers threw great, and we got beat in extra innings. After the game, our pitcher's aunt came to me and said she just couldn't take it. She couldn't handle to watch our guys play so well and get beat. What I said to her was, "You can't have great victory without the chance of gut-wrenching defeat."

I have seen people who would never give it their all because of the fear of failure. Have you fallen victim to the fear of failure and kept from laying it all on the line to whole-heartedly pursue the purpose that God has for you? Unless you totally commit to give it your best, you will never experience great loss, but you will never obtain the high give-up point and have the chance of great victory.

What is your give up-point on your child? Being a teacher I have seen parents with all kinds of give-up points. Some parents are more concerned about their own relationships, jobs, feelings, personal time, and their lives in general to commit to their children. I have also seen the other side when I thought, "Are they ever going to give up on this kid. He is a 21-year-old punk who needs to be cut off to learn a lesson."

Raising kids can be compared to combat in the respect that the harder you work with them, the harder it is for you to surrender in times of trouble. The more sweat you pour out raising them, the fewer tears you will shed on the fruits of their labor. You are also creating the cycle of life when you fully commit to your children's lives.

I am old enough now to see the cycle at work. Parents, whose own parents spent time with them, are now doing the same thing with their kids. The cycle of life goes on. Unfortunately, the cycle goes the other way, as well. I also see children with parents who are too busy, or just choose not to invest in the lives of their offspring. In most cases, these parents are just following the pattern that was set by their parents. What cycle of life will you set, or what cycle will you choose to break?

The same cycle of life tends to hold true in marriage. I always take a look at the parents of the boys my daughter dates. There is a country song that says, "I come from a long line of love." When mom is still married to dad, and grandpa is still married to grandma, the cycle of expectation has been set. Odds are they have come through the fire and learned how to become stronger.

My wife Shannon and I have had many things that have strengthened our marriage. We lived together in Fort Drum, New York at a time when I was gone often and worked long hours. Now, both of us coach high school athletics, and that poses a challenge with hectic schedules. However, I had no idea what going through the fire was until we lost a child. When you go through a challenge of that magnitude, your marriage will surely not stay the same. You will grow closer, or you could drift apart. I have grown to appreciate Shannon in a whole new way and will never give up on her or our children.

What is your give-up point? Stop and listen to God. He will give you what you need to set your give-up point where it should be—where He wants it to be. Even if you are in the position that we are with the loss of Jake, I will never give up on him. Continually I draw strength and motivation from his legacy. This book and the scholarship foundation are just two examples that I won't give up until I know my mission of serving my son's legacy is complete.

CHAPTER 9

Raise Children of Value Not Success

A friend of mine, Ricky Brown, came to my freshman health education class to talk to the students about insurance. Ricky is a very successful insurance agent, and before that had much financial success in the auto industry. The day he came to my classroom to speak to the kids about insurance he made a statement that stuck with me.

"I want to be a person of value not a person of success," he told the students.

What type of values are we instilling in our children? Are we leading them toward success or are we teaching them to strive for value?

I am sure you may have had this experience with your own children. Once when my daughter Jessi was about eight years old and Jake was about six, they both wanted to go out to eat. As a parent, you already know that this can be expensive, especially with my daughter, because she was raised on steak and baked potato. Honestly, I didn't think I had to ever worry about her dating because I didn't think any guy could afford her taste. This particular time, I told them we needed to eat at home and save the money. I said to Jake, "We need to save money and eat at home because we are poor." Jake being quick and witty came back with, "Dad we're not poor. We just don't have any money." I will remember that statement until the day I die because what Jake really said was don't place your personal value on the amount of money you have in your bank account.

How many times have you seen someone who has a bunch of money, but never really does anything of value or does anything to add value to others' lives? One of the things I tell our young student-athletes is, "Don't let playing time determine self worth." I have coached several professionals in my coaching career. However, they have been a pro in something other than sports. Our self worth should not be determined by money, fame, playing time or success. Rather, it should come from the value that we add to others by using our natural abilities for God's purpose.

We have to reinforce the right stuff if we are to teach our children to be people of true value. While reading an article in a magazine written about Pam Tebow, the mother of Florida football star and future NFL player Tim Tebow, one particular thing caught my eye. Pam would make her children go to the other sibling's sporting events and watch. Pam says this was to teach them that it was not always about them, sometimes it is about others. For four years, the whole country watched the fruits of her labor as Tebow and the Gators chewed up the competition on the football field. For his success on the football field, Mr. Tebow has gained fame and fortune. But as we continue to follow his career, I will bet the farm he uses that money and fame to add value to others and fulfill the purpose God has for him.

I had a young family come to me the other day and they had two of the most adorable children with them you have ever seen in your life. The little girl was signing up for basketball. She was 10 years old and her brother was eight. I started talking to the father, who was telling me about his kids and asking questions about the sports leagues in our area because they were from out of town. I could tell that both mom and dad were very proud of their children as they should be. We all are proud of our children most of the time. The dad was telling me how his son played in the football league where they came from and how well he did there. I mentioned how great of an education the children would get at our elementary school and that this was a wonderful place to raise children. Then, the dad started telling me how his son was a quarterback where they came from and he could throw the ball like Brett Favre. Sincerely, this was probably an exaggeration on dad's part. All I could do from that point on in the conversation, however, was look down at the little guy and think of Favre cutting loose a 65-yard pass off his back foot for a touchdown. I love sports as much as anyone and I would love to coach a kid who could throw like Brett Favre. It would make me look really smart. But as I walked away, I had to wonder to myself, are these young parents reinforcing the right things? Am I reinforcing the right things with my daughter, who is a very good high school basketball player? Things that I hope I am reinforcing are hard work, making everyone around you better, character, grades, Christian values and sportsmanship. But for anyone who knows me very well, my competitiveness sometimes may tend to supersede some of the other qualities I need to be teaching.

My daughter has a good friend named Whitney. Jessi and Whitney are now 16 years old, which as a parent should be very scary to you. Whitney plays basketball with Jessi and I help coach. I also have Whitney as a student in the Strength and Conditioning class I teach, so we get to spend a lot of time together. "Whit" has grown up coming to my house and playing with Jake and Jessi. Jake's favorite thing to do was agitate the girls. I am not sure where he got that from. In fact, Whitney was at our house the day before Jake died, and I had to break them up before they hurt one another. Jake loved her like another sister, and I love Whitney like another daughter. Maybe that is why we both have the inherent ability to get underneath the other's skin and at times drive each other crazy. A couple of times I have given Whitney some relationship advice when I thought it might be beneficial. She has no problem attracting attention from the boys. They think she looks like Taylor Swift. She has remembered on occasion a quote I gave her, "He who angers you, controls you." But the line she gave me was much better. Whitney said, "Dad told me it is as easy to fall in love with a rich man as it is to fall in love with a poor man." I thought that was profound and I have committed it to long term memory. Whitney's dad Jim and I are friends, and he was just kidding with her, of course. As a father, I know that Jim wants his daughter to marry a man that will support her, be loyal, faithful and raise his grandchildren in a good Christian home. We also want to teach our children to be people of value, not just people of success.

Take a moment to think about your children, your life and the people that you influence. Are you emphasizing things of value or things of success? What things do you reinforce? Is it character, compassion, honesty and integrity? Or is it high marks on a classroom exam, touchdown passes or three-point shots?

CHAPTER 10

Discipline is Important to a Child's Legacy

Other than the spiritual values that we instill in children, discipline may be the most important thing that we give them. Their intrinsic discipline sets them up for success or failure throughout the rest of their lives. Our goal as parents, teachers, coaches, or just as role models in general, is for young people to do what is right because it is the right thing to do. Discipline is something that is preached in every aspect of our lives. We want it and sometimes hate it, but without it we go insane. I believe much of the discipline we have as adults is instilled in us while we are young. It doesn't matter if it is the discipline to not talk in class, get up for work on time or study the Bible. The more we display discipline in our lives, the better chance we have to leave a worthy legacy.

Our pets are great examples of discipline. Right now I am sure some story is going through your head about your pet's discipline or lack thereof. Once Jessi had a boyfriend who bought her a dog. Well, most of you parents know how this story is going to play out; but I will tell it anyway. I refer to Pete as my grand dog after Jessi and her boyfriend broke up. I think that made Pete a step dog, but I am not sure. Pete's real name is Pistol Pete Nix after the late great Pete Maravich and the ex-boyfriend, who is a fine young man. When

Jessi leaves for college, I am quite sure Pete will stay with his grandparents. Many of you know how that works.

Of course, since Pete is part of the family now, he has to go to Jessi's rodeos. So we are in Memphis at a very nice indoor arena, and Jessi wants to take Pete inside to show him off and watch some of the calf roping—or the calf ropers—I am not quite sure. Pete has been on the farm a lot and he has seen goat tying, break away calf roping, been on cattle drives, and has seen cattle put through the chutes, so I am thinking this will be okay. Pete should have enough discipline to watch the calf roping without causing too much trouble.

Things were going all right at first. With the first two or three, Pete didn't mind the horse chasing the calf, but the cowboy getting off the horse and throwing the calf down and tying him up was apparently more than Pete could take. You would have thought that dog was straight from the main office of People for the Ethical Treatment of Animals (PETA) sent to represent the calf. Pete went nuts. He did not have the discipline it took to sit and watch calf roping. He was not ready for the type of exposure that we gave him. I wanted to give him a full attitude adjustment on the spot, but the fault was mine for taking him to something that he was not ready for.

If not careful, we can do this with our kids if we allow them to get into situations where they have to make a decision on what is right or wrong, when they are just not ready for that level of self discipline. As parents, it is our job to expose them to just enough to prepare them for the challenges that lie in wait for them. We shouldn't expose them to too much or to have too much freedom that would affect them in a negative way.

For the past 13 years, I have coached the high school baseball team in my hometown. We had seasons where we won 20 games, and we also won three district titles during that time. There were also some lean years—one in which we won only two games, and I am going to say we were proud to win two. That year we had four seniors who have all become very productive citizens. One graduated college with a 4.0 GPA. Even when our talent level was not that high, I still tried to instill discipline in the program and in the young men who were a part of it.

Every other year the team would travel to Ft. Walton Beach, Florida to play baseball. I required the players to have short haircuts, stay in uniform at the restaurant after a game, shave on game days, and gave the older guys more responsibility with team equipment than the younger guys. These things may seem a bit over the top to some people, but in all the trips we took to Florida, we never had a player get in trouble. We were not just representing ourselves; we were representing the team, the school, our hometown and our families. The baseball team had discipline, and it showed in the way we presented ourselves on and off the field. On the other hand, I have gone with school groups that are not part of a disciplined organization, and they are traveling just to be going on a trip. It reminds me of a quote from Sun Tzu in *Sun Tzu: the Art of War*. "Traveling with an army can be most advantageous. Traveling with an undisciplined mob can be most dangerous." We have had kids on other school trips bring alcohol and tobacco and sneak away to other locations. Not much should surprise you when traveling with an undisciplined mob. Hopefully, your home and your family vacations more resemble a well oiled disciplined machine, not an undisciplined mob.

When we discipline our children with their legacy in mind, discipline takes on a whole new meaning. When our kids are young, most of our discipline centers around not wanting them to get hurt or be disrespectful. It may seem tough to some people to spank or put a child in timeout for running away from a parent, but what if you are in a parking lot and they run and a truck hits them? Living on a farm, it is important to listen to things like, "Don't walk behind a horse. Stay away from the baby calf if mama doesn't seem happy. Don't go to the barn by yourself. Don't wrap the lead line around your arm." The list goes on. The goal for all parents is for our kids to do what we ask, not because they are scared, but out of respect for what is right. When I think about this, I think about my relationship with God. I want to do what He says out of respect, but there is still a bit of fear there, and that is okay. It is not a fear of you as a person. Your kids may have a fear of disappointing you or a fear of discipline.

The best example of how to discipline comes from God. He is not like Santa where you do your best and you will still get a present—a participation trophy if you will. The discipline we get from God is just, consistent and with the intent of helping us to leave a legacy of serving Him. We must not mistake every bad thing that happens in our lives as God's wrath. Preventing this from happening is done by constantly praying and seeking God's will in your life. Certainly one of the toughest things to do as a Christian is to distinguish between bad luck and God telling you to change directions. If you think you need to change directions, you better take a hard look at the situation because God will get your attention. God also disciplines us like we do our children, at first by guiding us to what is right and then toward leaving a legacy.

Unfortunately, all people don't learn at the same pace. Some of us are like my old dog Ty Cobb. He liked to chase cows in his younger days, but with one shock of the shocking collar, it's been 10 years since Ty has chased a cow. On the other hand, I bought Jessi a dog once that was supposed to be full blooded Shepherd. I'm not so sure. Dixie also liked to chase cattle, horses, cats and who knows what else. Dixie got many shocks from the collar, none of which changed her attitude about getting after livestock. She would just wait until you took the collar off. Dixie had to find a new address and a family who didn't own livestock. I could change Dixie's action, but I could never change her intrinsic attitude about chasing the stock. That is what we as parents all strive for—for our kids to have an intrinsic motivation to discipline themselves to do what is right. When we see our kids make choices because it is the right thing to do, we know we are raising a child that will leave a worthwhile legacy.

CHAPTER 11

My Heroes have always been Cowboys

Being raised on a farm teaches children and adults so much about life. There are so many moments that allow you to prepare children for things that they will experience later in their lives. The farm educates one about life from conception all the way to dying and death, and all phases in between. Work ethic and responsibility are two more qualities I have been able to impress on my children while raising them on a small cattle farm in western Kentucky. Jake and Jessi always enjoyed riding horses much more than working cows or helping with hay. But the cows pay the bills for our horse habit. Anyone who has ever been involved with horses understands that. We have raised cows on our farm since 1995. I thought I knew a great deal about them until I met Dan.

The first time I met Dan was when my daughter Jessi qualified for the Wrangler National Finals Rodeo when she was in middle school. As parents, we didn't know exactly what we were getting into at the time. The national finals were held at Red Rock State Park in Gallup, New Mexico. Parents who volunteered to help could get a free pass to all the events. This sounded much better than sitting around the camp all week, so I volunteered to help hang up sponsorship banners around the arenas. During the rodeo, parents from Kentucky were responsible for helping with calves in roping events. That is where I first met Dan. He was the stock contractor for the junior and high school national finals rodeo. That meant he either owned or contracted everything with more than two feet at the rodeo. The first year I was there I didn't get to know Dan that well, and I did not understand how this rodeo business really worked. One thing I realized immediately was that this guy knew what was going on. In every field there are those people you encounter and you say to yourself, "If I spend time with this person, I am going to learn a great deal." Dan was one of those people.

The next year Jessi made it to the national finals again and about halfway through the week, Dan asked if I wanted to hire on full time. It was just a few of us working the rodeo that year—Jerry, Dan, Dan's wife Linda, their son Dylan, Dylan's girlfriend Cheyenne, and me. This may sound like enough hands, but I quickly found out there was more to putting on a rodeo than most people will ever know.

Dan is an Okie. After college he started out teaching, but quickly found he could make more money as a stock contractor. He is a very good businessman and has forgotten more about cattle than I will ever know. He is also very impatient on the job and has no tolerance for bad cattlemanship. These qualities make him one of the most sought after stock contractors in the country. Jerry is one of the nicest people I have ever met. He is a very knowledgeable cattleman from south Texas and has become a good friend of mine. Dan's wife Linda is a great lady, whom Shannon and I love very much. The reason Dan hired me on in the first place was because if Linda had to work in the cow pens anymore with him, she was going to stop cooking or hit him over the head with a 2x4 or both.

Dylan and Cheyenne are both rodeo champions and have their own horse business in south Texas. One morning Dylan told me a story about how when he was at the Frontier Days rodeo he would get up early and sort the cattle before everyone else would show up. At the time I didn't really understand, but after a while it made perfect sense. It was my first real cattle lesson, which is that you must have everyone trained and on the same page with the same goals. If you don't have everyone on the same page with the same goals in your group, church, business, team or organization, people will set their own goals and it will be chaos. Dylan was a great teacher and helped me so much to understand how cows think and how to handle them properly.

What I have learned through my time working at the rodeo with these great cowboys is that if you can handle cattle, you can handle and lead young people. The principles of working with cattle and working with kids are so much alike, it's not even funny. I have put together my top 10 list of "If You Can Handle a Cow, You Can Handle a Kid."

1. <u>You have to think like a cow</u>. This may sound too simple, but it is true. How many times have you heard an adult say, "I just don't know what that kid was thinking?" You have to understand their mentality, their values and what motivates them. Just like God's thoughts are higher than our thoughts and His ways are higher than our ways, the same is true between most adults and kids.

2. <u>Cattle have a natural flow</u>. If you ever look at a field where cattle have traveled, you will see trails through the field. Kids have a natural flow too. I heard of a university that built a new building on campus. They did not put in any sidewalks to the building. A few months later, the contractor came back and looked for the dirt paths so they would know the best place to put the sidewalks. When you set up working pens for cattle, you take into account the fact that cows always want to go to corners. Things like this make the environment safe and happy for the cow and the cowboy. How do you know if the natural flow is not working? It's evident if more than five percent slip or fall, if cattle are vocal in the chutes, if you have to use an electric prod on a high percentage on cattle, if cattle move faster than a trot, or if they run into gates or fences going 90 mph. Every day I see examples of this teaching in a high school building that was designed in the 1970s. I would venture to say that over half of our discipline problems—tardiness, bullying, fighting

and skipping classes—are in some way caused or averted by controlling the natural flow of the students. If students think they are not going to get chicken nuggets because they are too far back in the line, they are going to cut line or run to the chow hall. The hallways are too narrow at the school, and the natural flow always leads you through the wrong door. Some of these things we can't change, but some we can if we just understand the natural flow is the shortest path with the least resistance.

3. <u>Cows think about one thing at a time.</u> Kids, on the other hand, can go either way on this one. Some kids are just like cows. They have one thought at a time, and those come kind of slow. Others must have at least 10,000 different thoughts per minute. If you have ever worked with someone who is ADD or ADHD, you know what I mean. It's not that they can't pay attention to one thing, it is that they pay attention to everything. One example I see all of the time is many kids of this generation are able to focus better with music. Most older people like me need total quiet to read or study because that is what we are accustomed to. I think a lot of kids are allergic to the quiet. Just check out your house and see how much quiet time there is without some kind of background noise or entertainment.

4. <u>Cows think the closer you are, the smaller you are and the farther away you are, the bigger you are</u>. For example, one person can move a pen of cattle down a thirty-foot wide alleyway pretty easily if you keep your distance, keep the herd moving and make yourself big. But if you get too close to the herd, you will become smaller to the cattle and one or ten of them will decide to turn back and you have a mess. Kids may not think like this physically, but they do socially. People whom they don't know that well, but look up to or admire, seem bigger than life to them. In school, we use this concept in a mentoring program for older kids to be a positive influence on younger kids. We also have to be careful because this concept makes us think that outside help may always be better. The truth is that most kids just need quality time with their parents. Our tendency is to think an expert is someone from out of town with a briefcase. Sometimes

this might be true. My wife's uncle Jerry told a funny story one time that shed some light on the theory of hiring an expert. Jerry was working for a major oil company when a very high dollar and large piece of equipment broke down. He was pretty sure an employee at the plant could fix the problem. But the company wanted to bring in this "expert" from England. After several days and a lot of money spent on the expert, they still had the problem and the Brit had headed home, but forgot one thing—his briefcase. Well, the old engineer at the plant fixed the problem; but just like you and me, they had to know what was in the briefcase. I am sure it took some time to get the case open; but when they finally got into the expert's personal case that he had packed all the way from England, they found that it contained just a sandwich and a banana. Wonder if the company thought they got their money's worth? Don't sell yourself short. If you spend time with kids and you care about them, they will trust you; and you will have the greatest impact because you are the expert, whether you feel like one or not.

5. <u>Cows want to move away from pressure</u>. That is, most cows will move away from pressure. Others will try to stomp, kick, hook, butt, and otherwise convince you to stay away from them. Kids and adults are much the same way in that they may move away from pressure. That is not to say that we don't like the pressure of a job or the pressure of competition, but we will probably try to avoid unnecessary pressure. Usually we will follow the path of least resistance. This can be good or bad depending on the situation. The bottom line is we must use pressure to achieve positive results. Some of the best workouts that our football team does are when I can set up a hard workout that has a time restraint and a difficult but achievable goal. When I can work with them, cheer them on without prodding and they just kill themselves to make the goal, I know I have set up a productive workout; and I have used pressure not as a threat but as a positive tool.

6. <u>Cows want to move to other cows</u>. If you have ever tried to drive one cow away from the herd, you know what I am talking about.

Kids want to be with other kids, and our job as parents is to make sure they are in a safe, positive and supervised environment.

7. <u>You can work cows quietly or rawhide them</u>. I learned from Dan and Dylan the best way is to work them quietly. Rawhiding them like in some old western movie may look good, but it does nothing but detour the profitability of your cattle operation. Even though there are times when you have to rawhide, you want to keep it to a minimum. I tell parents to pick their battles and win the ones they pick. Don't pick too many because you will wear yourself out. When the kids were little, I would take them somewhere; and when I would get back, Shannon would always ask, "How did they act?" I would respond that they were good; they are always good for me. She would then say that is because you let them do what they want, but my response was that I just picked my battles. From a dad's perspective, combing your hair, wiping your nose and taking a bath every 24 hours are not battles that I always choose to fight. Another good way to avoid rawhiding your children is to simply state what you want them to do, not what you don't want them to do. At first glance you are probably thinking this is a no-brainer. Next time you go to your local Wal-mart, just listen to how people talk to their children. Some examples might go like this: "Stop that running . . . Don't touch that . . . I'm gonna whoop your butt . . . Stop that yelling . . . or Quit acting a fool." I will be to first to admit that a dusting off of the hindquarters at times will do a wonder of good for the attitude. But statements like "Use your inside voice . . . Walk in the store please . . . or Point but don't touch" might sometimes help you avoid having to get to the point of rawhiding your children. Jake would love to tease his mom and tell her she was all talk and no action, then he would just look at her and grin. He really knew better, but for him it was a great way to push his mom's buttons and get a bit more of her attention. The truth is we have all seen parents who are all talk and never follow through with discipline. And any child, ages two to 18 years old, can figure this out quickly and use it to their advantage. A much better approach is that of Theodore Roosevelt, who suggested we "walk softly and carry a big stick."

When dealing with kids or cattle, the figurative stick is not for beating, but rather for reproach. For our children, as well as for ourselves, there has to be consequences to our actions.

8. <u>One crazy one can ruin the herd</u>. One summer that I worked for Dan the crazy one was No. 44. He was a nut. He ran over Shannon in the alley way. He jumped out of the working area and ran through the RV parking. I can't even begin to tell you what he did to the little cowboys after they roped him. As soon as possible, Dan put No. 44 on a truck to the pro rodeo for some special training. At our own farm here, No. 8 was the crazy one. She had good calves and was a good mama; but any time you tried to get the herd up, she was gone and her calf and half the herd would follow her. It didn't take very many times of this happening before we gave her a new address. How does this relate to kids? You better know who your kids are hanging out with. I work with kids every day that I love to death, but when it comes to making good decisions, I don't trust them any farther than I can throw them. One crazy one can get the whole group in trouble.

9. <u>Cows all have a bubble</u>. We have a 1,800-pound bull on the farm named J.R., and his bubble is about 5 feet. If you stay outside his bubble, all is well; but when you invade his space, he starts pawing the dirt, shaking his head, snorting and slobbering all over himself. Needless to say, not many people invade J.R.'s bubble. Kids are the same way. They all have a physical and emotional bubble. I wish some of them had a little larger physical bubble. But the emotional bubble is the one you must be able crack to make a difference in their lives. This takes time and trust. Remember, you are the expert, and you can do it.

10. <u>Cows are always watching you—especially when you have them in a pen</u>. Kids are always watching you as well. One of the things I love about coaching is that the kids hold you to the same standards you hold them. My players are always watching what I eat, what I drink, the language I use, and how I support the administration of the school. They may sometimes be slow

to do what I say, but they are always quick to imitate what I do. We have all seen our kids imitate us. In 2010 Shannon and I welcomed our third child into the world. One example I have really enjoyed is having a baby and a 17-year-old daughter together in our home. Shannon is a great mom, and it has been great for Jessi to get to watch her mother model how to raise a baby. Jessi will ask all the time, "Did you do that with me?" And when Jessi thinks we are not watching, she will do the same things with Jordyn as Shannon does. At times it will be easy to see, at other times it is harder; but kids are always watching, and we are always leaving a legacy through them.

CHAPTER 12

Prom Dresses and Pacifiers

On May 13, 2010, we were blessed with the birth of our third child, Jordyn. Whether to have another child was a question that we had personally dealt with and is a question that many couples ask themselves. Of course, there are lots of factors that need to go into this decision. Can we support a child? Do we want another child? Why do we want another child? When we bring another life into this world, there are many risks and no guarantees. But I also understand that without high risk, we can never have high reward in sports or in life. So, as you pray and listen to God about bringing another life into your family—whether it is by birth or adoption—I hope this chapter will give you some things to consider.

Before the loss of Jake, I would have never considered having another child. In fact, not long after Jake was born, I was so sure that I didn't want any more children that I had a vasectomy. I did learn a good lesson in this process. The bottom line is, if you are going to have a procedure and you live in a small town, do some research beforehand, or see a specialist from out of town. I did neither, and it left me in a rather embarrassing situation. For whatever the reason, I thought this minor surgery was going to be just me and the doctor, who was a friend of mine, and no one else in the room. That was the wrong answer. When I got in there, along with the doctor were about five nurses who all knew me, and I knew them. Some of the ladies I just knew in the community, but I had one of the ladies' daughters in my health class and another's son played baseball for me. You can only imagine the conversation the next time I saw those kids. "Hey Matt, I saw your mom the other day . . . ." I will let you fill in the rest. At least there were not any high school students doing career shadowing that day. Once again, I prove that I am not very smart. But, as you know, if you have any medical procedure in which you get morphine, after enough of that goes into your system, you don't care what they do to you or who watches.

For Shannon and me, the decision to try to have more children was a very emotional one. We spent much time in prayer and talking to each other. I listened to God and my wife, and sometimes I am not sure in which order because many times they come together. Twelve years before, I was the one who was too selfish and worried about how we were going to pay for everything to want any more children. But now I have a totally different view of why we have children. Many people offered us their thoughts, shared books and bits of inspiration after Jake's death; but there are two things in particular that I look back on that really directed me toward having more children. My friend Jamie told me about a conversation he had at work. One person asked how someone could think about bringing a life into this world with all of the troubles and pressures they will face in this country and this world. Another Christian person was quick to reply with "How can we change things without raising Godly, moral children of character?" Obviously, I am not suggesting that we all start having more children, but we can all make a difference in the lives of children no matter our age or situation. Children will make a difference in the world as I have witnessed in the events that transpired following the loss of my son.

Finally, Shannon and I decided we were going to attempt to have more children. We knew that it was not going to be an easy road, but we knew God's direction for our lives. The first stop was Shannon's doctor to make sure it was as safe as possible. I was then referred to Nashville to a well-respected urologist. This was my first visit to a urologist's office, and it was quite the experience. The people there were so nice to us and very considerate of our situation, but the one thing you have to remember is that the people who have to visit the urologist all have a problem, and most are older. After consulting the urologist, he recommended we go to the Nashville Fertility Clinic to look at options and see if Shannon's ovaries were still healthy enough to have children with minimum risk. The normal wait at the clinic is about 30 days, but they were able to get us in that day. Fantastic news—my wife is an ageless wonder because of very little use of birth control. Her ovaries looked great. While at the NFC, we experienced something of a turning point. We were able to laugh for the first time. Not much, but we did experience some personal healing. So if you need a good laugh, I would recommend you visit the urologist and the fertility clinic in the same day. What a paradigm shift. You go from old people with old people problems to young people with a whole different set of problems that mostly center on wanting to get pregnant. I am quite sure this was a turning point for both of us. We went from a family that laughed and played together all the time to one who couldn't laugh at all. In public, I even felt guilty if I smiled because I was supposed to be sad, and most of the time I was.

Grasping the concept that we are put on this earth to glorify God and inspire others is not just a theory, but one we need to remember and strive to live by. Speaking for myself, Jake and Jessi have both inspired me to live with a higher purpose, put others above myself, be a better husband, better dad, and to challenge others to live a life that will leave a legacy. It doesn't matter if we live to be 12, 40 or 97; we will be judged the same. What did we do to glorify God and inspire others on a daily basis? With that said, after much prayer and counsel, we believe children are not only fun and inspiring; but also a way to touch others. After returning from Nashville, we began to try to have children. This can be big news in a small town, so it was kind of awkward when people would come up to me and say, "I heard Shannon was pregnant." My response was "not that I know of," or "I don't think so". After about a year, we were both a bit discouraged; but we knew that was what we were led to do, so we decided to go back to Nashville to look at options. We went for a consultation and then came home to wait for an appointment to start fertility treatment. There must have been something in the water, because after just visiting that place Shannon was pregnant. On May 13, 2010, we went to Paducah and brought home Jordyn Anna-Marie Hodge. She has been such a blessing and a lot of fun for all of us. I didn't know how it would make us feel, or if it would help take any of the hurt of losing Jake away from our hearts. At this point, the hurt of losing Jake has stayed the same. We still miss him just as much as we did. We still get sad and cry, but the joy that is created in a new life has been great. I saw a lady at the Dollar General one day buying a pacifier. I asked about her baby, and she told me she also had one going to the prom that night. Just want to let you know that it's not bad to have one with a pacifier and the other in a prom dress. It's a lot of fun.

Fourth Quarter Comeback

Without the chance of great loss there can never be great victory. This relates to almost everything in our lives. It could be our jobs, our children, and the games we play. The harder you work, the harder it is to surrender. That is why great games are made when two teams are battling for a championship and neither of them will give up. Great lives, careers, legends, and legacies are made from the same formula. The picture that comes to my mind that illustrates this is of the great man Winston Churchill chewing on a cigar, looking like a little bulldog and saying, "Never, never, never, give up." He had everything to lose if he was not successful, and everything to gain if he was. Never give up on a fourth quarter comeback, whether it be finding that special someone or a new job, winning the game, or finding happiness again after the loss of a loved one. God has a plan for you; and as my friend Lieutenant John P. Drohan told me while we were training for the Best Ranger Competition, "God writes straight in crooked lines." It may not be clear now, but if you keep looking, you will find your purpose and make the comeback God desires for you.

It is important to note that four years have passed from the time I started this book until now. My hope is that it will be a blessing and a unique perspective on dealing with loss, as well as be a testimony to how I have been able to work toward making a physical and emotional comeback. One of the things that you should take from this gap in time is that your own comeback may not happen as quickly as you desire. It will not happen on your timetable but rather on God's timetable. This can prove to be very stressful because in the game of life that we play, it seems God has a lot more time than we do.

Within a few months' time, our little community lost several prominent citizens. One of the men I work with lost his daughter and another coworker lost her husband. This has given me some insight into how people felt around me during the days after Jake died. I wanted to help them feel better, but I found myself not knowing what to say or do. One thing that helped me during this time was the stories people told me about my son, so I have tried to use this in talking with people going through similar circumstances. The lady who teaches with me who lost her husband recently, was the wife of Dr. Dennis Lacy, former superintendent of Crittenden County Schools. I wanted to share the following story with her to show how important her husband had been to me, and to help her remember how others enjoyed his personality. After I got out of the army, her husband gave me my first job back home. Dr. Lacy, or Doc, was a role model and a mentor to me. He was also a big Rocket football fan. When I was playing football in 1985 for the Crittenden County Rockets, we were getting ready to play Carroll County in the semi-state game. The winner would go on to play in the state championship. Doc loved to tell a story about Carroll County's superintendent. Carroll County had a good quarterback, and their superintendent was quick to tell Doc how great he was and how well he could throw the football. Doc asked him, "How good is he at throwing from the prone position?" The gentleman asked, "What do you mean, Doc?" Dr. Lacy replied, "How is he at throwing from sitting on his butt because that is where he going to be all night." The other guy didn't see the humor, but Doc thought that was hilarious. We backed up his trash talk with a 35-7 victory and intercepted their quarterback four times. And the young quarterback did spent a lot of the night on his butt. Our team also went on to win the Class A State Championship that season. So, my point is that retelling little stories like this one about Doc and reassuring those experiencing a loss that it will get better are sometimes all we can do to share in the grief of others. I remember what that meant to me.

We all have our favorite comebacks. I am a huge sports fan, and being from Kentucky, one of my favorite comebacks occurred in 1994. The Kentucky Wildcats were down 37-68 to the LSU Tigers at LSU. The second half saw the Cats outscore the Tigers 62-27 to win the game 99-95. St. Louis Cardinal Fans will all remember game 6 of the 2011 World Series. The Cardinals trailed the Texas Rangers 7-4 in the 8th inning, 9-7 in the 10th inning, came back to win the game in the 11th, and then went on to win the 2011 World Series. NFL football fans know about "The Drive." John Elway took the Denver Broncos 98 yards in 5:02 to score a touchdown that forced overtime and helped lead the Broncos to victory against the Cleveland Browns in the 1987 AFC championship game. If you are a sports fan, right now you are probably thinking about your favorite comeback, when your team snatched victory out of the jaws of defeat.

Comebacks are not limited to a particular game. At some point, all of us must stage comebacks in life. The comeback in life is certainly not as quick, and it can be very difficult; however, it's a great opportunity to display our faith. In my life, our whole family has had to make an emotional comeback. We will never get over the loss of Jake, but through his life and death we feel we have been able to help others. As you are reading this book, your comeback may be in progress. A friend of Shannon's and mine has been a very successful division I women's basketball head coach for several years. She had a great career at a major university as a player and a coach. She was very involved in community service always willing to help others. After two subpar seasons she was fired this spring. Though things are tough right now, she will make a comeback. I am quite sure God has a very straight plan for her life, though it may seem a bit crooked right now.

I started being a Yankee fan when I was about seven because my dad was a Dodger fan, and they played the Yankees in the World Series. If you are old enough, you will know what I am talking about when I say that I can remember going out back of the trailer where we lived and turning the antenna until my dad said to stop. We could pick up NBC out of Paducah and watch the game. I wanted to root against my dad, so I became a Yankee fan and have been for about 35 years.

Just a couple of days ago the greatest relief pitcher of all time, in my biased opinion, Mariano Rivera tore his ACL while catching fly balls during batting practice. Mariano is a man of strong faith, but in an interview after the news that his ACL was torn, he was in tears and uncertain of playing baseball again. But only a few hours after the first interview, he sent out a statement that he would make a comeback to baseball. Only time will tell of his performance, but his faith and character gives strength to anyone who knows him.

Over the past four years the Hodge family has fought to make a comeback and live our lives in a way that might honor God. We have had successes and failures; nevertheless, we feel tremendously blessed. In 2011 with Shannon coaching and Jessi at the point guard position, the Crittenden County Lady Rockets won the Class A regional title. Additionally, that season we won the regular District and Regional titles. In the state of Kentucky this is a really big deal because we have an unclassed system of regular basketball playoffs. That means our school of 375 students competes against schools of 1,500 or more students, along with private schools that can take students from anywhere in the state. Even though we were defeated in the state playoffs, it was like the movie "Hoosiers" for us to even make it to the Kentucky high school Sweet Sixteen Tournament. Jessi has since gone on to play college basketball and earn a 4.0 GPA during her first semester, something I never accomplished in my many years of college. Jessi is also dating a young man whom we all love and who treats her with the respect that a young lady deserves. Coincidentally, he received a football scholarship to a school about a mile from the school she attends. Funny how that happened, don't you think?

Also, Shannon has found the passion to coach again. For a long time it was hard to go back into the gym. And it is still difficult at times, but I know that is what God would have her do. Now I again am able to be myself around her most of the time. This by the way means annoying the crap out of her, in a very respectful way, of course. As I have already discussed, there has been a new addition to our family. We took a chance and followed our hearts and now we have another gorgeous daughter. In just a few days from writing this, Jordyn

Anna-Marie Hodge turns two years old. Not only is she a blessing to us, but a lot of fun. She looks like Jessi and acts like Jake. A friend of mine who had kids later in life told me that when you are in your twenties and your children mess up, you whip them; when you are in your thirties, you put them in time out; and when you are in your forties, you say "Honey, grab the camera." My friend is completely right. Jordyn keeps us laughing. We will do our best to raise her with the same character and religious values as our other children, and I pray she will leave a legacy.

I have started coaching basketball again. This past season was my first season as the head boy's varsity basketball coach. It has been a great experience and a lot of fun. Things were tough without my point guard. It was the first time I had coached without Jake at the point in a long time. That was and is an adjustment. The team has a new point guard now. His name is Aaron, and he was one of Jake's best friends. We both experienced a bit of stress adjusting to our new roles, but I think it has been a blessing for each of us. Aaron has done a great job leading the team. Jake and I always had the dream of him playing and me coaching the team while playing in front of a packed house. I still share part of this dream, but it no longer has anything to do with myself. Now the pleasure I get from coaching comes when I see young men accomplish something they have never done before. From my perspective, I can walk away tomorrow, or I will coach as long a God tells me to stay in this position. Leaving a positive and lasting impression on young men is the most important thing I can do.

Another part of our family's comeback has been the foundation. We created the Jake Hodge Foundation. The JHF provides $1,000 to students going to college. The foundation's mission is to help students who display honesty, character, and integrity in their actions. The foundation rewards students who excel in the classroom and in their chosen field of competition. Our goal for these students is that they be challenged to lead a purpose driven life and leave a profound legacy. Our goal for the foundation was $100,000. As of this writing, we have over $90,000 and should reach the goal this year. Another step for me in the healing process has been this book.

Jokingly, I tell people I am writing a book and they don't have to read it because it's not very good, but it is on my bucket list. Maybe it will be a blessing to others.

With God's guidance, we feel we have been able to make a comeback from our biggest loss. It hasn't been easy. All of us have had to work at it very hard, and each of us has experienced setbacks. If you have had a big loss, you must stop and listen to God. He will give you purpose. I see a lot of kids come through our football program. Many are very dedicated to Rocket football. Unfortunately, when that is over, a few sometimes have trouble finding another purpose in life. Of course, we coaches try to guide them in the right direction; but at the end of the day, the responsibility falls squarely on the individual kid's shoulders. You may be experiencing the same thing at this very moment. You may feel like you have no purpose any more. You may have poured everything into your job, a relationship, a child, or a business; and without that, you feel like you have no purpose or cause for a comeback. This is not true for you. God always has a purpose for you. You are useful to Him, and you can make a comeback.

Difficulties will come, the winds of adversity will blow, and the devil will tell you that the best times are behind you. Don't listen to the negative thoughts. Never, never, never, never give up on living a life of service and happiness. It will get better!